Accelerated Learning
Made Easy

Dale Owen

© Copyright 2019 by Dale Owen

All rights reserved.

The following book is reproduced below with the goal of providing information that is as accurate and reliable as possible. Regardless, purchasing this Book can be seen as consent to the fact that both the publisher and the author of this book are in no way experts on the topics discussed within and that any recommendations or suggestions that are made herein are for entertainment purposes only. Professionals should be consulted as needed prior to undertaking any of the action endorsed herein.

This declaration is deemed fair and valid by both the American Bar Association and the Committee of Publishers Association and is legally binding throughout the United States.

Furthermore, the transmission, duplication, or reproduction of any of the following work including specific information will be considered an illegal act irrespective of if it is done electronically or in print. This extends to creating a secondary or tertiary copy of the work or a recorded copy and is only allowed with the express written consent from the Publisher. All additional right reserved.

The information in the following pages is broadly considered a truthful and accurate account of facts and as such, any inattention, use, or misuse of the information in question by the reader will render any resulting actions solely under their purview. There are no scenarios in which the publisher or the original author of this work can be in any fashion deemed liable for any hardship or damages that may befall them after undertaking information described herein.

Additionally, the information in the following pages is intended only for informational purposes and should thus be thought of as universal. As befitting its nature, it is presented without assurance regarding its prolonged validity or interim quality. Trademarks that are mentioned are done without written consent and can in no way be considered an endorsement from the trademark holder.

Contents

Speed Reading

*****

Introduction 1

Chapter 1: What is Speed Reading? 3

    The Basics of Speed Reading 3

    The Benefits of Speed Reading 8

    Do Speed Reading Programs Really Work? 13

    Does It take long To Become a Confident Speed Reader? 14

Chapter 2: The Speed Reading Shortcut – Steps to Make Speed Reading Easier 18

    Stop the Subvocalization 19

    Figuring Out your Current Starting Point 20

    Using Indicators 21

    Focus on Control 23

    Doing Exercise Minimizing Eye Movement 25

    Skipping Small and Unimportant Words 25

    Using Programs for Help 27

Skimming and Scanning 29

Consistent Practicing Schedule 30

Chapter 3: Calculating Your Reading Speed 32

Calculating your Reading Speed 33

Average Reading Speed 35

Words-Per-Minute 35

Chapter 4: How to Read Faster 40

The Hand Pacing Technique 40

Scanning and Previewing 43

Reading Groups of Words 49

Eye Exercises to Improve Reading Speed 52

Chapter 5: Where People Go Wrong with Speed Reading 60

Common Mistakes with Speed Reading 61

Myths with Speed Reading 66

What If I'm Not Improving with Speed Reading? 68

When and When Not to Use Speed Reading 69

Chapter 6: Comprehension When Speed Reading 72

How Speed Reading Affects Comprehension 73

    Retaining More Information during Speed Reading 74

    Techniques to Help Comprehend Better through Speed Reading..78

Chapter 7: Subvocalization.............................. 87

    Best Ways to Minimize Your Subvocalization 94

Chapter 8: Practice Makes Perfect..................... 99

Chapter 9: Speed Reading Studies 113

    Be Careful with Sites that Try to Sell You Speed Reading Programs...113

    Additional Studies about Speed Reading............119

    Knowing When to Slow Down 123

Conclusion... 127

The Unknown Methods of Critical Thinking

✳✳✳✳✳

Introduction 130

Chapter 1: Understanding Critical Thinking ... 132

    What Is Critical Thinking? 133

    What Are the Critical Thinking Skills? 138

    What Critical Thinking Involves 140

    Qualities and Characteristics of Critical Thinkers 142

    Examples of Critical Thinking 148

    Thinking Hiccups 150

    How Can Critical Thinking Benefit You? 153

    Can I Really Use Critical Thinking? 156

    The Main Components of Critical Thinking 157

Chapter 2: Critical Thinking Test 164

    The Critical Thinking Test 164

    How Often Should You Test Yourself 171

    Different Types of Thinking Tests 173

Are Some Tests Better Than Others? 174

How Can I Tell If I'm Improving? 175

How to Identify Critical Thinking Issues 176

Chapter 3: The Steps and Stages of Critical Thinking 181

What Are the Different Stages of Critical Thinking? 181

    The Unreflective Thinker 182

    The Challenged Thinker 183

    The Beginning Thinker 184

    The Practicing Thinker 185

    The Advanced Thinker 186

    The Accomplished Thinker 186

What Are the Different Steps of Critical Thinking? 187

    Knowledge 189

    Comprehension 190

    Application 191

    Analyze 192

    Synthesis 193

    Take Action 194

Chapter 4: How to Develop Your Thinking Skills 196

Ask Basic Questions 196

Question Some of Your Basic Assumptions 197

Being Aware of Your Mental Processes 199

Try Reversing Things 200

Evaluate the Evidence That You Have 201

Always Think for Yourself 203

Not Always Needing to Think Critically 204

Chapter 5: Questions to Apply in Critical Thinking 206

Knowledge 207

Comprehension 208

Application 209

Analysis 209

Evaluation 210

Creation and Synthesis 211

Chapter 6: Decision-Making 212

What Is Decision-Making? 212

Things That Can Affect Your Decision-Making 217

How to Make a Decision 219
    Determine What You Have at Stake 219
    Why Are You Making the Decision? 220
    Determine the Number of Choices You Have 221
    Make Your Decisions Informed 221
    Consider a Second Opinion 222
    Decide with Logic and Leave the Emotion Behind 223
    Learn from Your Bad Decisions 223
How to Make Better Decisions 224
Decision-Making in the Workplace and Life 225
Techniques to Improve Your Decision-making Abilities 228
    Stop Delaying 229
    Put the Emotions and Ego Away 230
    Always Question the Data You Have 230
    Understand the Risks 231

Chapter 7: Problem-Solving 233
What Is Problem-Solving? 233
Why People Struggle with Problem-Solving 238

The Process of Problem-Solving 243
Problem-Solving in the Workplace and in Life . 247
    Brainstorming 247
    Delegation 248
    Committees 249
    Evaluations 250
Useful Problem-Solving Skills and How to Develop Them 251
Techniques to Develop Your Problem-Solving Abilities 253
    Focus Less on the Problem and More on the Solution 253
    Adapt the Five Why's 254
    Simplify as Much as Possible 256
    List out as Many of the Solutions as you Can 257
    Think Laterally 257
    Use Language That Opens up New Doors 258

Conclusion 260

Memory Improvement Mastery

✹✹✹✹✹

Introduction 262

Chapter 1: Understanding How the Mind Works 264

    The Brain and How It Works to Memorize Things 265

    The Flaws of the Brain and the Mind 269

    Memory Consolidation 272

    Why and How We Forget and Remember Certain Things 275

        Attention 276

        Consolidating the Memory 277

        Memory Recall 278

        Priming 279

        Mood Memory 280

        Blanking Out 280

        Duration Neglect 282

Why Some People Remember More Than Others 283

What About Photographic Memories 285

How Age Can Affect the Memory 289

Chapter 2: What Causes Memory Problems 294

Possible Causes of Memory Problems 294

Identifying Memory Problems at Home, Work, and in Relationships 298

Are You Burnt Out Mentally? What Are the Signs? 301

Remembering Names and Faces 307

How Focus, Concentration, and Observation Affect the Memory Process 310

Memory Recall 312

Let's Test Your Memory 319

Chapter 3: Memory Improvement Techniques and Exercises 323

Stop Multitasking 323

Focus Your Attention 326

Avoid Cramming 327

Be Organized and Structured 328

Relate the Information Back to Things You Know 329

Read the Information Out Loud 330

Trying Meditation..330

Live a Life That Is Blessed and Happy 333

Getting Enough Sleep 336

Playing Brain Games..338

Master a New Skill 341

Trying Mnemonic Devices...............................343

    The Method of Loci....................................344

    Acronyms 345

    Rhymes 346

    Organization and Chunking.........................348

    Imagery 349

The 4 Details Exercise......................................351

Number Brain Exercises...................................352

Doing Recall in Your Mind..............................353

The Metronome Clapping Exercise 354

Create Your Own Memory Palace 355

Learn a New Language.....................................356

Working with a Mind Map 358

Playing a Sport 358

Chapter 4: Memory Improving in Your Day to Day Life 361

Exercising 362

Socializing 363

Mental Activities 364

Organizing Your Life...................................... 365

Eating Well 366

Sleeping Well 368

Medications That Can Help with Memory Improvement 372

Chapter 5: Rebooting and Refreshing Your Brain 375

Mindfulness 376

Visual Tasks 377

Chewing Gum 378

Belly Breathing 379

Conclusion 382

Speed Reading

By Dale Owen.

Introduction

In the following chapters we will discuss everything that you may need to know to get started with speed reading. Speed reading is one of the best life skills that you can learn. It will help you to take in more information quickly, allowing you a chance to communicate better with others, and also improve the time in which you can work.

You will also find with speed reading, that reading will actually become a much more enjoyable experience rather than an arduous task.

This guidebook is going to spend some time talking about speed reading and how it can benefit you in your daily life. We will take a look at what speed reading is all about, how you can benefit from speed reading, some of the different techniques that come with speed reading, common mistakes, and even how to increase your comprehension during your speed reading sessions. That is one of the neat things about speed reading. It isn't just about seeing how fast you can get through a page. When you work on it slowly and try to improve your reading speed at a gradual pace that works for you, your comprehension levels of the material will actually also improve aswell.

We will also spend some time talking about subvocalization and how it can be the number one reason that you can't increase your reading speed and see results. Then this guidebook will end with some information on how to improve your reading speeds and some case studies to show you just how effective speed reading can be for your needs.

There are so many great benefits to speed reading. It can enhance your personal and your professional life and is one of the best skills that you can work on for yourself.

There are plenty of different books on this subject available on the market, so thanks again for choosing this one! If its not too much trouble, id like to kindly ask if you could spare some time to leave an honest review once your finished, thanks!

Chapter 1

WHAT IS SPEED READING?

Reading is an activity that can engage a lot of different parts of the body including the brain, mouth, ears, and eyes. When we talk about speed reading, we are looking at a process that is able to engage these senses even more than normal. You will learn how to use the senses, as well as your brain, more efficiently and powerfully than ever before. Speed reading has many different factors to consider when implementing, and getting the most out of your reading times, can make a big difference in the experience you have. Let's take a look at what speed reading is all about!

The Basics of Speed Reading

The first step that you will take when you are ready to read anything is to take a look at the words. But how do you see the words that are on the page when you are reading? Before the 1920s, it was believed that individuals would just go through and read out one word at a time. They thought that to read, you had to move your eyes from left and then over to the right, going across the page. This required you to take in one word after another. With this theory, individuals who were faster readers were simply those who could see and recognize words faster than others.

However, even as a beginner in reading, you can see and then read more than one word at a time. Reading isn't just a smooth transition or flow. You will move the eyes across the page, but it is common to see a lot of jumping ahead in more of fits and starts, taking in between one to five words at a time with just a quick glance. This is normal reading behavior, even though we may not even realize that we are doing it.

The neat thing about speed reading is that it is able to take these natural stops and goes, and clustering of words, and turns it into a method to help you read faster. You already read several words just with one glance. This is true even in regular reading. You may only stop if you come across a word that you don't know as you try to figure that one out.

Speed reading will also help you to expand your vision. Most people who don't use speed reading can take in between one to five words. A speed reader could take in twenty words or more with a single glance, which is why they are able to get through something so much faster.

The expanding of the vision isn't just vertically though. You will find that with speed reading, you are able to expand out your vision to read horizontally as well. In addition to being able to take in more than one word when you read some text, a speed reader has worked on the ability to read and understand the words on different lines, all in the same glance. Isn't it amazing what our minds can do with a little bit of time and practice!

When you read, you may find that you speak the words to yourself. This can be done out loud or in your head. This is the way that we are used to reading things because we were taught the sound it out a method of reading in school. We were taught how to sound out letters and do combinations to read out any word we saw. When we are able to sound out these words, we can learn how to read better.

The problem with this approach is that it is going to slow you down when it comes to reading. You are going to read more at the speed that you talk, rather than at any other speed. Sounding it out with words is fine for those just learning how to read, but it is important to learn when to get rid of this so that you can eventually read faster. People usually don't speak very fast, so using this as your limit to speed reading means you will be done without improving anything.

When you say and hear the words that you are reading, this is going to be known as vocalizing. Vocalizing is something that you will have learned way back when you first got started with reading, which may have helped you in getting started. But it is time to abandon that when you are ready to be a speed reader. One of the things that you will need to work on when learning how to speed read is to shut off that internal vocalization, so it doesn't slow you down.

Another thing to consider is that speed reading is all about comprehending what you read. How well you are able to comprehend what is going on in the document is going to be determined through a variety of factors including how familiar you are with the subject matter, how big your vocabulary is, and your reading speed.

You may be surprised to learn that speed reading is actually a method you can use that will increase reading comprehension. Because you will learn how to read a few words at a time with this method, you will have better luck with learning the meaning of words based on their context. Speed reading, due to this fact, can have a big effect on the size of your vocabulary and your general knowledge, which then turns around and increases your reading speed.

All forms of reading are going to require you to concentrate. Some will require it for longer than others, but to get the message out of the writing, then you need to be able to concentrate. You will find that with speed reading, it is required that you have a sustained, forceful concentration on the material. This is because you are doing a ton of things at the same time, and by doing this effectively, you need to have a good amount of concentration.

To speed read well, you need to see and read the words that are in front of you. Remain alert to the main ideas that the author is trying to send out to you. Learn how to think in the same manner as the author, and detect the method she uses to present the material. That way, it is easier to find out where they put the main ideas. You also need to be able to read with a type of perspective to separate out the details from some of the heavier and more important things. You also need to be able to tell when you can skim, when you should read fast, and even when you need to slow down so you can catch more if you get confused.

Speed reading is one of the best ways to increase your productivity, ensure that you have something to talk about with others, help you to stay on top of changing industry standards, and so much more. It may take some time to learn more about how to use it, but it can definitely be an asset to learn the skills that go with it.

The Benefits of Speed Reading

Speed reading can actually be very beneficial to you. It isn't just about showing off to others that you can read through the newspaper or a document or a book in no time at all. It is also a way to help you comprehend what you are reading and helping you retain the information more effectively.

There are many ways that speed reading can help to improve your life. To start with, many people who properly use speed reading find that it can do wonders for improving the memory. The brain is just like any of the other muscles in the body. If you spend time training the brain, it is going to get stronger and will be able to perform better. One of the neat things about speed reading is that it is going to give our brains a challenge, forcing it to perform at a higher level than usual.

When you use speed reading as a tool to train the brain to take on information faster than before, you will find that all areas of the brain are able to improve, including the memory. When you use the memory in reading it can act like a stabilized muscle. When you speed read, it is going to get in a good workout as you move along, helping you to improve the memory all in one.

Another benefit that you may be able to enjoy when it comes to speed reading is better focus. Reading speed is calculated by words per minute (also known as wpm) The average reading speed for most people is about 200-300 wpm, but in some cases people that speed read can hit a staggering 1200 words per minute. But why is there such a big gap between these groups?

There are two main reasons why we find this kind of gap. The first one is that the reading styles that we are taught when we were younger are not the most efficient. The second is because we lack focus. While we can't do much about the way we were taught to read, we can try to override them with some of the techniques that we will discuss later on. But if we can't focus on what we are reading in front of us, our minds will start to wonder, and we will easily think about other things rather than the content. Speed reading can help build up the focus instead.

Some people often find that when they become an experienced speed reader, they are able to increase their levels of self-confidence. This may be because you can learn anything that you want in a short amount of time with a good level of speed reading skill. Sure, it won't be an absolute amount of learning, but it could be enough to help you prepare when you need to talk with or meet with someone new. This can keep you from stumbling along for topic ideas, and also make interactions with others much easier.

When you take the time to improve your ability to read, and therefore learn, faster, you will find that a lot more doors are going to start opening up for you because there are more options in your life. This is since every book or articles, regardless of whether they are nonfiction or fiction, can help us shift our awareness and we may be able to see more in depth about our lives. This is going to help us see a boost in our own self-confidence.

Reading is a very good exercise that you can do for the brain. When you train the brain not just to read the words, but also read them faster, something amazing can happen. The brain will become more efficient when it is time to sort through information and find correlations to other information bits that you stored in the past.

The more that you are able to improve the reading speed, the faster this process is able to happen. As a side effect of this, you will start to notice some big improvements with logic because you get used to responding quickly to what before would have taken a lot longer to process.

And finally, reading can help improve your personal and emotional wellbeing. Reading is relaxing for most people in general. It can help to reduce the amount of stress that you have because it ensures that you are able to get your mind off your worries, and of the other thoughts you have that may not be beneficial or healthy.

When you can reduce the stress and hide the negative thoughts, this will help you to focus mostly on the information that you take in through reading. This can be a form of meditation that is known as an active meditation. With this type of meditation, you get the same benefits of normal meditation and get into the same kind of state, but whilst doing an activity. It also provides you with an increase in emotional wellbeing and a release of tension.

Speed reading isn't just going to be about learning how to read faster. Think of it more like an exercise. When you exercise the brain, just like you do with your muscles, it is going to start getting significantly stronger over time. This can provide you with all of the benefits that we have stated previously.

Do Speed Reading Programs Really Work?

Speed reading is something that interests many people. They often want to increase their speed, but at the same time avoid wasting time trying to get through all the content they are trying to read. When you first start looking through some of the options for speed reading, you will encounter tons of different options online that promise to make you fast at reading in just a few weeks, or even less. These types of promises sound attractive to people and usually tempt people into trying them.

However, there can be some problems that come with this. First, many of these programs cost a lot of money. They make big promises that they will be able to help you read in no time, but often these promises do come with really big price tags, sometimes in the thousands of dollars. But is it really worth this much to increase the speed at which you are able to read?

Many times, these courses are going to fail. They won't be able to teach you anything. Sure, you may feel like you are making some progress, but you do all of the work on the computer screen with words flashing at you and praising you for not actually doing that much.

Then, when you go back to trying to read a regular document, your comprehension and your reading speed start to go down again.

Even with the programs that are successful at helping you to increase your reading speed, you will find that all the techniques that they teach you are the same ones that we teach inside this guidebook. While these techniques are really great and can increase your speed, the programs that cost hundreds or even thousands of dollars aren't much more impressive overall, and just cause you to throw lots of money away.

Speed reading may be a skill, but that doesn't mean you have to pay a premium to get the benefits out of using it. You can utilize your finger or a pen and a variety of reading materials and do well. Add in some methods that help you count how quickly you are able to read through, so you can test yourself on occasion, and you are set to go.

Does It take long To Become a Confident Speed Reader?

When you first get started with speed reading, you are probably really excited to see your reading speed increase and go to new heights. You are excited to see some of the benefits that come with speed reading and how it can benefit your life. But one question that you may still have is how speed reading actually is going to work and how long it takes to see improvements.

There are some factors to consider when it comes to speed reading. Everyone is going to progress at a different rate. Some people may have more time to devote to their practice, and others may find it hard to sit down and practice at all. Some people may have a pretty fast reading level to start with, while others may start out at a slower pace. Understanding what goes into speed reading and why it may take you a bit longer to reach your success, or your goal, compared to others, can help you to make the best use of your time and can give you a good idea of how long it will take to see the results.

The first thing to consider is your current reading speed. If you are already considered a fast reader now, then you will progress through the speed reading techniques faster than others. You may already know some of the methods and are using them in your own reading already, but now you just need to improve upon it a little bit more to get better results and to become even faster.

But then there are those who are slower readers. It takes them a long time to get through any type of reading assignment and maybe they even feel miserable when they have a large book or document to read through. These individuals will have to practice more, and it may take longer for them to get the results they want with speed reading.

And of course, some people fall everywhere between these two levels. Your reading level when you start can have a significant influence on how successful you will be with speed reading and how long it will take you. Don't compare yourself to others here because you never know where they started out. You may be behind a few people, but you are so much further ahead of others as well.

Another significant determinant of how long it takes to do well with speed reading is how much time you dedicate to practicing, and how consistent you stay with it. If you sit down and spend half an hour each day on some of the techniques that we discuss in this guidebook, and you work hard on your speed reading, you will find that you improve very quickly. But if you only devote a few minutes here and there or you only practice once every few weeks, you are not giving yourself the practice that you need to do well.

If you want to see some great results with speed reading, you must make sure that you give it the time, attention, and practice that it needs. This ensures that you are going actually to get enough practice so that you can get better. The speed reading progress isn't going to happen just because you want it to. It will happen because you dedicate yourself, and remain consistent, with the work that needs to be done.

Speed reading can benefit you in so many ways. It can help you to communicate with people more intelligently. It can help you to be more educated and informed about the information that is the most important to you. Learning some of the best techniques to speed up your reading and to help you take in more information can be one of the best life skills that you learn.

Chapter 2
THE SPEED READING SHORTCUT – STEPS TO MAKE SPEED READING EASIER

Speed reading doesn't have to be a process that is hard and complicated to work on. In fact, you may find that it is a straightforward process if you take a moment to learn about it. Many people may feel that they will never catch on to the secrets that come with speed reading, and that they should just give up now before they end up making themselves tired and frustrated. But in reality, a few minutes a day, along with some of the techniques that we will talk about in a bit, can be enough to ensure that you will see some results with how quickly you can read through various materials. This chapter is going to provide you with some shortcuts you can take, as well as the best steps, to make your speed reading a reality.

Stop the Subvocalization

This is the hardest thing that you are going to work on when you get started with speed reading. Because of the way that we are taught how to read, we often limit ourselves because we think out the words that we are reading, rather than just reading through them and comprehending them. What this does is slows us down to only being able to read as fast as we can talk. This keeps us around 250 words per minute and no more, which is definitely not speed reading.

How can you do this? A good trick to work on is to pick out any word in any text that you want, and then look at it for a moment, staying silent. There may be a bit of subvocalization that comes with it because that is what we are used to, but by merely taking in words without the desire to pronounce them, we are practicing the skills that we need to help out with this problem.

After being able to do this with individual words, just taking them in without the need to pronounce them or sound them out in our heads, you will start to form a new habit of taking in the word and understanding it, even if you are moving faster. It may take a lot of practice, but over time, you will be able to limit the amount of subvocalization that occurs when you read.

Figuring Out your Current Starting Point

Another element that you need to consider when it comes to working with speed reading is the ability to recognize when you have grown and are doing better than before. Before you are able to figure out this growth though, you need to be able to measure your reading against a baseline. This means that you need to test your reading speed before you even begin, and then test it again at consistent intervals during the training to see how you are doing.

There are a lot of great resources online that you can use that will help you track these results. For example, ReadingSoft.com works well because it will provide you with a quick and consistent measurement of how fast you are reading through some material. When you regularly take reading tests, whether it is through that site or another one, you will be able to see when you are improving your skill, and this is often the motivation that you need to keep things going.

The problem that comes with understanding your own baseline is that it becomes hard for you to translate it into practical terms when you see how many words per minute you are able to read. It is a great place for you to start, but from a practical view, it is important to know the number of minutes it can take to read through a page.

For most people, it can take about 5 to 10 minutes to get through a single page. But for a speed reader, two or three minutes can be enough. This means that for a speed reader, a book that is 200 pages long should take them about 400 minutes to read. But for the average reader, this same book could take between 1000 and 2000 minutes to read. The average reader will spend an extra 13 hours reading a book than a speed reader would, which adds up to a tremendous amount of time which ideally could be reduced.

Using Indicators

We are going to talk about this one in a bit more detail later on, but it is one of the best techniques to use when you are practicing your speed reading. Using a finger to make sure that you are guiding yourself is something that we see a lot of children do as they learn how to read, but since you are learning a new skill as well, it is definitely something that you can utilize too.

The pointer is useful for pushing you along more than helping you keep your place. It is easy to become fixated on a word or phrase when we are reading, and then this slows down our time. When we set a pace with our finger, we force ourselves to move along, without looking back at all, so we can keep up and increase our speed.

The guide needs to be moved at a pace that is very consistent. You never want to go through and stop the finger or try to slow it down. It simply needs to slide from one side of the text over to another at a uniform speed. When you practice using your pointer finger in this manner, you will notice that any time you get stuck or lose momentum much easier than if you simply tried to follow along and move as quickly as possible.

When you just try to go through things and move as quickly as you can, the fluid motion that you need to attain while speed reading isn't possible. You are eventually going to hit a limit, and you will end up skipping words. This causes backtracking, and that results in a lot of confusion. If you do this just two times on each page, it could add in 30 seconds or more per page, or an additional 100 minutes for a book that is 200 pages. That is an extra 90 minutes to finish a book. Just by learning how to reduce how many times this happens, you can increase the speed at which you read by.

Focus on Control

When you are moving through your text, you may find that there are certain parts of the book that are easy for you just to breeze through, but then there are some that are much too full of information that you will need to learn, causing you to slow down and take it all onboard. This is a pretty natural part of reading, and being able to transition smoothly from the easy to read material to the thick material is something that you need to learn how to control. Always remember that speed isn't the only important part of speed reading. You must also take the time to do the actual reading as well.

Let's take a look at two different books to help you see how this works. The first book that we will look through is a thick and boring textbook about history. If we wanted to be able to find specific dates and names inside of this book, it would be pretty easy just to speed read through all of the pages and then scan for the information that we need. If we wanted to find out the significance of the dates and the people, we would skim until we found the information we need, and then slow down to learn about those people and dates. This is a measure of control that we need to work on.

With the second example, the book is going to be one of fiction. This is more about a whimsical story where a family has become trapped on a mountain, and the story follows all the adventures that they have whilst they try to stay clear of danger. Because the brain enjoys this fictional piece, there is no real reason to have much control over this process of reading, unless we find that we don't understand some part of the story. We can go through the text pretty quickly and let the story fill up our mind. If we feel there is something significant or something we missed out on, then we can choose to slow down if we think it's needed. Otherwise, we can just keep reading through the material at any speed that we want.

Doing Exercise Minimizing Eye Movement

One of the biggest things that you can do when you work to speed read is to learn how to minimize the number of movements your eyes make when you are reading. If you are able to start paying attention to how often the eyes are moving when you read, then you will be able to help limit it a bit. This can add hours back to the reading experience and can make the reading time easier to handle.

There are a lot of different exercises that you can work with when it comes to helping your eyes to get stronger and to work on how many movements the eyes need to do. When you do these exercises, you are able to isolate the core components of using your eyes to speed read. You can get more words into each glance, and can also prevent backtracking overall so you can make your reading speeds faster.

Skipping Small and Unimportant Words

To help you figure out the best way to become a speed reader and how they are able to get through pages so quickly while the rest of us struggle, it is important to realize that not every word on the page is equal to each other. There are a lot of smaller words on the page that help with grammar and are important to make sure the sentence flows, but they don't really add much to the sentence at all. For example, take a look at any sentence and remove the words "The, An, A, And." You can still read through that sentence and get the understanding of what is inside it.

If you are able to learn how to eliminate all of these small and irrelevant words, you will find that you are more effective at getting more out of the page and fully understanding what is going on with that page. When you skip these small words, they are not translating to anything that is useful. This allows you to spend more time looking at the information that you need, rather than wasting it on all those small words. And since many times, those small words take up half or more of the words on the page. When you are able to eliminate them, imagine how much more you are able to get done in a shorter amount of time.

The process of training yourself to skip these small words is as simple as recognizing that you don't really need to pay all that much attention to them. Simply allow the eyes to move across and not focus on those unnecessary words. This can take some time, to do. You have to train your eyes to skip over these words, which isn't as easy as it sounds as we are used to seeing them and reading each of them. Over time though, with some practice, your brain is going to learn how to skip over these words for you naturally. This allows you to just read the most important words on the page causing you to read that slight bit faster then usual.

Using Programs for Help

While you shouldn't spend a lot of money on these apps and programs because you can do a lot of the work on your own, you may find that using a few speed reading apps and programs can help you out. The best tools that you use for speed reading are simple, common apps that are going to help you streamline the process of learning the skill.

There are a few options out there to choose from. Most of them are going to provide excellent features that make using them both an exercise in speed reading, and a way to save time. One option that you may like if you use IOS 8 is the Accelerator. This one is able to import documents, articles, and any other texts and links that you need into the speed reading practice app. This helps you practice and learn because you are adding in articles that you already are looking at reading, which can make the practice much more engaging and entertaining.

Another option is to work with Spreeder. This is a tool that will help you to copy and paste any kind of text that you want into its small word processor. The app will then take whatever has been pasted and turn it into an exercise so that you can pick and choose what you would like to read and practice all on one app. Spritz App can be a good one as well because it doesn't work the same with teaching you how to read faster. It works to use the software to reconfigure the things that you want to read in a new way. This one is more about not moving the eyes. It is going to flash the words in front of the eye, highlighting one letter to center the word to keep the eyes tracking as they flash by fast.

These are just a few of the options that you can choose. But look around and find one that is free or very inexpensive. These are just supposed to be tools in helping you out. The options that promise to be full courses are often not effective and can cause issues with spending too much and not seeing the improvements as you would like with your reading skills.

Skimming and Scanning

Two main methods are used when it comes to speed reading. The first one is to use your pointer finger or another tool to help move you along and avoid issues with fixation. The second one is skimming and scanning. We will take some more time to look over this as we progress through this guide. But basically, you will use some different techniques to help you get through the text faster, stop reading each and every word, and still get the meaning that you need from the text.

Skimming will allow you to search for some of the main keywords that you need to get through the text faster. If it is a topic that you already know a lot about, then you can simply look for the main topics and keywords that are needed to understand the material. You can then glance through the material and find these important parts and see if there is any new information or something that you may need to focus more of your attention on, rather than having to read through the whole thing.

There are a lot of different things that you can do when it comes to skimming and scanning to get the most out of work. You can take some time to preview the material, such as looking at any summaries or taking a look at the front or the back cover of the document, such as if its a book. You can choose to look at the chapter headings and the subheadings along the book to see what topics will be discussed. Some people even find that reading the first few paragraphs and then just the first lines of each paragraph can help them to get enough information without needing to read each word.

Consistent Practicing Schedule

If you have come this far in the speed reading process, well done. You already have all the tools and the information needed to get a handle on the process and work on developing your skill. It may seem in the beginning that speed reading is a really difficult skill to master, but it isn't as hard as you may think. With just a few key parts being understood and a lot of practice, you are sure to get this all mastered in no time at all.

From this stage, your biggest goal is going to be to find regular and consistent times to continue practicing the techniques that we talked about above, and that we are going to talk about in the rest of this guide. You don't have to give yourself a ton of time to master these skills. But if you never practice at all, or just practice a bit here and there and never on a consistent basis, you will struggle to improve this skill at all. Even fifteen minutes a day can be enough to enhance your reading speed and can make this a skill that is easy to utilize.

Chapter 3
Calculating Your Reading Speed

Before we get into some of the techniques that you can use to increase your speed, it is important to have a basic idea of how fast your reading speed is in the beginning. How are you supposed to know how far you have come in all of this if you don't know where you began? This chapter is going to take some time to look at how you can calculate your own reading speed. There are also a few different options you can find online that can help you do this automatically.

Once you do the reading test, make sure that you keep the number somewhere safe that you can find later. At regular intervals, whether it's every week or each month which ever works best for you, take another speed test. You can then compare the two numbers and see how far you have come. This is a great way to keep you on task with your speed reading goals, and when you get stuck or feel like you aren't progressing, you can compare these numbers and see how far you have really come.

Calculating your Reading Speed

Here we are going to give you a simple formula that is easy to work through to figure out your reading speed. You also have a choice to use some of the tests online to figure out your reading speed if you so choose. The steps that you can use to figure out your own reading speed, and to see where you are starting this journey include:

- ❖ Take out a document or a book or something else to read. Turn on a timer for five minutes and just read at your normal pace.
- ❖ When the time is up, mark the spot where you stopped.
- ❖ Count the number of words that are found in the first five lines that you read. Divide this number by five, so you get the average words per line.
- ❖ Then Count the number of lines that you read.
- ❖ Then Multiply this by the number of lines that you read by average on each line. This is a

rough estimate of how many words you have ended up reading during that five minutes.
- ❖ Now Divide it by five, so you know how many words per minute you were able to do.

Since this one doesn't have a set number of words for you to read through, it may be a little bit off. But it is a good method to go with to teach you how these words per minute are calculated. You can also choose to pick out a document with a known number of words and then time how long it takes to read that normally. Divide the total number of words by how much time it took to get your words per minute.

The goal is to see if you can get faster than this first time. Write that number down someplace safe, and then, when you have had some time to practice and get better at speed reading, you can go through the above test again and see if you have gotten faster. You may be surprised by how much you improve each time that you do the test. Keep records so you can always look back and see how far you have come.

Average Reading Speed

For most people, the average reading speed is going to be about 200 words per minute, or slightly higher. This allows them to comprehend what they are reading, but it also shows that quite a bit of subvocalization is going on as well. Some readers are able to get around 300 words per minute, but this number is pretty low.

The goal is to get yourself to 1000 words per minute or more. If you are done at 200 words per minute right now, this may seem like a crazy goal that you will have trouble meeting. But even those who read at a slower speed can use speed reading to improve their skills. You can start out at any level, and using some of the techniques that we will talk about later will help improve your speed. Even if you just can't manage to get to 1000 words per minute, improving your reading speed by even a couple hundred words per minute can make a big difference.

Words-Per-Minute

There are a lot of different reading speeds to watch out for. Sometimes it depends on what level of reading you are at (beginners are going to be slower at reading compared to older adults), and other factors. Below is a good idea of what a word per minute can mean depending on the level you are at:

- ❖ 1 to 100 words per minute: This is the speed that we often see beginners and children reading out. This is considered the borderline of literacy. There is little recollection or even understanding of the material that is read. But the person is beginning to read, so it usually gets better.
- ❖ 100 to 200 words per minute: This one is going to still fall below average, and many people who fall in this range find that they don't enjoy the reading at all. It is difficult for them to read to learn and stay up to date on any changes occurring around them. Many times, their comprehension of the material will still be under 50 percent, even if they are older.
- ❖ 200 to 250 words per minute: Many people are going to fall somewhere between this range. This is the average speed for reading. But if you are re-reading the words and trying to subvocalize them, then your reading

comprehension can still be down at fifty percent.

- ❖ 250 to 300 words per minute: This number of words per minute is going to be just a bit above range, and there are a lot of post-high school graduates that will use this kind of speed. But you will find that the comprehension will still stay around fifty percent.
- ❖ 350 to 500 words per minute: This is the range that is above average by quite a bit, and the ones who fit into this category of speed are the ones who typically enjoy spending their time reading. The retention of these individuals can be good, and it falls somewhere between 50 to 75 percent. This is good reading speed, but you will find as we go through this book, you can do much better.
- ❖ 500 to 800 words per minute: This is fast reading speed. These individuals enjoy reading quite a bit and are starting to fall into the speed reading category. These people are often the ones who will spend their free time curled up with a book rather than watching a movie.
- ❖ 800 to 1000 words per minute: This is efficient reading speed. You should be able to use this

speed and not have to feel pressured or stressed about reading. You will understand lots of words and their meanings well, and you may have even spent some time doing speed reading training along the way. You don't waste your time subvocalizing words or re-reading them.

- ❖ 1000 words per minute or faster: You have now entered the speed reading area. Being able to read at this speed means that you now have complete control over your reading and you are a master of it. This is considered an elite reading category. Reading is a big part of your life, both for business and for pleasure, so reading at this sort of speed will be highly beneficial to your life in general.

So, the first thing that you need to do here is to take some time to test out your reading speed. You can pick an online test, or you can use the steps that we talked about above. Don't try to speed through the reading or do anything unnatural at this time to try to impress anyone. Doing this is going to mess with your results and makes it hard to see where your baseline truly is. Simply start out by reading at your natural speed and then you can see where your current reading speeds are at.

If you find that your reading speed is a bit lower than you thought, or on the lower end of the spectrum above, don't fret, or be too harsh towards yourself. There is plenty of time to work on your speed reading and to improve it a lot more. You simply are doing these tests to figure out how to speed yourself up; it doesn't really matter how fast or slow the reading is in the beginning. Speed reading can help you to increase your speed, and even if you just increase it by a few hundred words a minute, you will find that your love of reading, and how quickly you can get through things, will increase as well.

Chapter 4
How to Read Faster

Once you have spent some time to look at you reading speed and you know where you want to start, and maybe even have a goal that you would like to reach with this process, it is time to learn some of the techniques that are needed to help you read faster than ever before. Let's take a look at some of the different techniques that you can use to go from your current reading speed to a speed reader in no time.

There are actually quite a few different techniques that you can choose to go with when you want to increase your reading speed. All of them can be effective, but it often depends on who is reading and what works the best for them. Some of the best speed reading techniques that you can try out include:

The Hand Pacing Technique

This is such a simple method to use, and you only need your own hand to get it done. This allows you to read faster while ensuring that you read at a steady pace, so you can get through the document without getting distracted or stopping at different words. Have you ever worked with or heard about someone using the pointer method? Most of us learned how to use this technique when we were in school, but many of us dropped the habit as we got older. But even as of today, it is still an incredibly effective method to use.

Working with hand pacing is pretty easy. You just need your hand, or your finger, and some sort of document to work with. When you are ready and comfortable, you can use these steps to help you get used to speed reading in this way:

- ❖ Sit down at a 45-degree angle from the document you are reading. Sit as comfortable as possible, and have your elbow on the table.
- ❖ Let one of your hands hold onto the reading material. Then you can use a pointer or the index finger on either hand, whichever is the most comfortable for you.
- ❖ Position the pointer under the word that you want to first start with. Start pacing yourself as you read through the document, moving along

the lines and making sure you never fall behind the pointer.
- ❖ Keep your eyes concentrated on both the pointer and the words that show up in front of you.
- ❖ The pointer needs to move at a steady pace the whole time that you are reading and doing this exercise. Do not let it slow down and don't let your eyes or the words determine how fast you get to go. The pointer or the finger get to choose the pace.
- ❖ Try to remember what you can from the document. If you are struggling with comprehension, then you can adjust the speed. But always strive to go faster each time that you practice.
- ❖ With this method, make sure that you just keep moving. It is fine if you miss a few words here and there. If you are catching most of the document, then this is not going to be an issue. Just keep going, even if you do miss a few words.

When you work on this, your motion should be free-flowing and continuous. If you know the material is going to be more difficult, you can go at a slower pace to help with comprehension. But don't let the pointer slow down just because you feel like it. Coax the brain into going faster and allow it to handle the words and everything else. If you get back into your old habits and notice that you are not self-pacing any longer, just start again!

Scanning and Previewing

Another method that you can go with is the scanning and previewing method. This one will enhance your skills when it comes to capturing the central idea of what you are reading, without wasting time going through all the introductions and all the other stuff that might get in the way. When you use this technique, you may focus your attention on things with lots of information that is condensed so you will learn how to look at subheadings, indexes, graphs, points, and lists to find what you want.

Scanning is a technique that you can use that will trigger and then extract key information and ideas from the document, without having to read the whole thing. You will use scanning simply by moving your eyes quickly down the page, looking for either specific phrases or words to help you get the main idea of that document. You can also use this as a way to figure out whether a source is going to be the one that will answer your questions or not. In many cases, you can use this to get a lot of information out of a document, although not full comprehension, in just a few minutes.

Skimming is a little bit different. This one works well with nonfiction material, and it helps you to focus on the main concept of the document. You will figure out what is the most important parts to the document that you can read. You can choose to stop if you find something that is particularly interesting to you, but the point is to keep on moving and getting through the material.

Previewing key sentences

There are actually a lot of different skimming and scanning strategies that you can use to help increase your reading speed. The first one is going to be previewing key sentences. For this one, you will find the sentences that are at the beginning of a chapter or a paragraph. These are going to give you the basis of what is going to be found in the rest of the writing without having to read through all of it.

Each paragraph is usually going to spend its time on just one idea, though there are sometimes when the paragraphs are going to relate to each other. When you are able to skim and then find out the central idea that is behind each one, you will be able to get the basis or the gist out of it, which aids you in understanding what is in the whole chapter, just by reading a few lines.

You can also go with an approach that is slightly different. You can just look for the information that you need, and then skip the rest. This can help you to read the first and then the last sentence of those longer paragraphs. When you read these two sentences, you learn what the paragraph is about, and how it is summarized. This gives you a ton of information with just a few lines, enabling you to move on to something else quickly.

Scan for any numbers and names

For pretty much every text that you are going to work with, you will find numbers and names inside. These are there to tell you more details about the concepts, places, and people you should pay attention to. There is no order of getting that information in a text during a preview. However, you will find that you can understand some of the main facts of a document, or gain a better understanding of where and when a story takes place or who is involved when you look at numbers.

Scanning for trigger words

The concept with this one is to preview a text, maybe using some of the techniques above. But your goal here is to look for important words that seem to be critical to the document, or ones that seem to keep popping up as you go through the text. Mainly you are going to find compounds or nouns when you are doing this. Some of the trigger words that you may look for will include key sentences, places, names, and numbers.

Reading the title

Always take the time, no matter what method you do, to read through the titles. The title, the content, and the back of the book or text is the most important thing that you can do. This helps prepare you for what will be found in the rest of the document, and may even be able to reveal a few of the trigger words that you need. You can go through and read the titles of the chapters, the headings and subheadings, and any short summaries that show up.

Exercises for skimming and scanning

This is often one of the best techniques that you can use for speed reading when you want to take in a lot of information quickly, without wasting your time and without needing to have a lot of comprehension on the material. Some of the ways that you can practice working on skimming and scanning include:

1. **Key sentence:** For this one, go and grab any book that you like. Take a moment to read through the first sentences or the first few paragraphs that are there. Now try to recall the ideas that your mind grabbed and latched onto when you read through those sentences using the concept that we talked about above. As a beginner, just do this on about four to five sentences. Once you have mastered it on that amount of reading, you can jump ahead and do more.
2. **Names and numbers:** For this one, you can choose any article that you want. Then skim through it and see what numbers or names you are able to find with it. When you find a fact, a number or a name, pause for a few seconds, not very long, and realize it. You can choose to say

the word out loud if you would like. Now, start reading through the entirety of the document and see if the facts, those that you paused on, will start to reveal themselves as you go.

3. **Trigger words:** For this one, you can choose a few different books or articles to get started with. When you have them ready, you can start by reading the titles, the content, the back of the book, and any headlines that you see. From this information, try to write down a few trigger words. When you start speed reading, stop at the words that interest you. Write those words down as well because these are new trigger words to pay attention to. When you are done, see how much information you were able to comprehend from those articles.

Skimming and scanning are great options to go with if you want to be able to read through a lot of information quickly, without having to worry about comprehending everything. This helps you to get the gist out of the information, so you can share the news, or know what is going on, without having to read each individual word.

Reading Groups of Words

Out of all the methods, reading chunks of words is considered the most advanced out of all the techniques. You can also combine it with the others, such as pacing, to move faster. When you use this particular technique, it is going to make it easier for you to process big chunks of words, rather than just going through and reading out the single words that are there. It has been used by many people to fully process the information at hand, rather than having to go through and read slowly through each individual word.

Learning how to read chunks of words is all about training, and it can take some time. You have to learn how to expand out your vision, so you can read a chunk of words at once, and get their meaning, rather than just one. Some of the things that you will need to practice when it comes to reading groups of words include:

- ❖ Extend the vision
- ❖ Combine a few different reading strategies
- ❖ Reduce some of the other bad habits that you have formed when it comes to reading

- ❖ Ignore some of the filler words that are there, but don't really contribute to your comprehension.
- ❖ Learn how to focus your attention mainly on verbs and nouns.
- ❖ Reduce any stops that are due to eye fixation.

As a beginner, you will want to start out with just chunking together two or three words at a time. While this method can definitely help you become a faster reader, it is sometimes difficult to do. You can go through and just chunk together two or three words in the beginning, and you will instantly see how much faster it is to read. Over time, you may be able to glance down and read a whole paragraph in that single glance, and only take just a few seconds to do so.

The training plan for this one is pretty simple. You can set aside about ten to fifteen minutes a day to help you learn how to recognize many words at the same time while reading. Don't make the training session much longer than this, or implement other methods besides just chunking. This can be a long period, especially for beginners, to spend on just speed reading techniques and can wear you out.

When you start your training, work with just two words chunked together at a time. This is the perfect place to start as a beginner, and it is going to stimulate the brain to process a larger number of words each minute. You don't need to rush or skip up a level until you are able to read the two words at a time smoothly and easily.

You can also add in the pointer method here. Using your index finger to help you go from one group over to another can make it easier to jump around the page without getting fixated on any word. You can also use the pointer to help you go a bit faster to get more stimulation and to ensure that you will be ready to move onto the next level in no time.

We will talk about this in a bit, but you may notice that the issues of subvocalization show up as a beginner to speed reading, which may be the thing that is slowing you down quite a bit. What this means is that while you are doing these exercises, you are trying to pronounce the words in your head, or even by moving your mouth, while you read. This is a bad reading habit that is pretty common, but if you want to progress chunking five words or more, it is one that you need to be aware of, and you need to work on to avoid.

After you master at least four words chunked together in a sentence, you can try to use a hand pacing method that is known as the Zig Zag. With this method, instead of following the lines perfectly, you would go down the page in a zig-zag motion, jumping to different word groups each time. The point of this is to help you skip past all of the words that are just filler, helps you to move faster, and an ensure that you get to the central idea of the document or book much faster than before.

These are some of the main methods that you can use when it comes to increasing your reading speed. As you can see, the ideas are pretty simple, but they will require you to do some work. Even ten to fifteen minutes a day as a beginner can be enough to stimulate the mind and teach it how to read in this manner. Over time and with some persistence and dedication, you will be able to become a speed reader in no time.

Eye Exercises to Improve Reading Speed

In addition to some of the techniques that we discussed above, you should also consider working on your eye movements and eye strength as well. None of the methods that we talk about are going to be that effective if you can't move your eyes fast enough to read through the page and if you aren't able to take in more words at a time with the help of your peripheral vision. Luckily, there are a few different exercises that you can do with your eyes to help you with your speed reading includes:

Thumb-to-thumb glancing

This first method is a good one to use to work the eye muscles and help you to control your peripheral vision. It can also stretch out the muscles of the eyes to make them more flexible and healthier. To work with this kind of exercise, you should glance at your thumbs without moving the head at all. The steps that you can do to work with the thumb to thumb glancing exercise includes:

1. Sit or stand, whichever is the best for you, and look straight ahead without turning your head at all. Then stretch the arms out to your sides, letting the thumbs stick out.
2. Without letting the head turn at all, glance back and forth between the left and the right thumbs, doing this ten times.

3. Repeat these steps a few times to work on the peripheral vision and to make your eyes stronger.

This is an exercise that you can add in at the beginning of each of your practices to ensure that you are able to see your eyes get a bit stronger. It only takes a few minutes at most, and you will start to notice a lot of improvements to your reading speed in no time.

Eye writing

The second exercise that you can work with is known as eye writing. With this exercise, you are going to move your eyes in ways that it may not be used to working with. The eye gets used to seeing things in a certain way. These muscles are well trained, but you may want to strengthen them a bit with the help of moving your eyes differently than they are used to. This gives them a workout, and may make the muscles a little bit sore in the beginning, but can be really worth it for improving your reading speed.

The eye writing exercises that we are going to talk about will work on the extra-ocular muscles that are in the eye socket, and it is perfect for helping increase the amount of flexibility in the eye as well as its range of motion. It is a simple process though, you just need to use the steps below to help you get started:

1. Find a blank wall that you are able to do this with. Try to sit across the room from it, or as far away as you can from that wall.
2. When you are ready, stare at the wall and imagine that you are writing your name on that wall. You will move the eyes around as you would with a paintbrush like you were writing the name that way.
3. You can try writing out your name in a few different manners. You can do it in block letters, uppercase and then lowercase, and even in cursive.

You can do this with any kind of word that you want. Only do it a few times the first few exercises that you do it to help you get the basics, but your eyes will get tired in the beginning. Over time, you will see improvement, and you will find yourself being able to do more complex words, and for a longer period of time. This is another one that you can bring into the beginning of your speed reading practice to ensure that you stretch the eyes out a bit and can help you read a bit faster.

Hooded eyes

Now we are onto the third exercise that you can work on. This exercise is going just to take a few seconds, and works the best when you have been speed reading for a bit, and you need to give the eyes a little break from work. Sometimes we get into some of our speed reading a little too much, but then our eyes get tired and worn out in the process. Hooded eyes are a great way to relax your eyes a bit so that they don't strain too much, and you can use it in the middle of the practice to help you keep going for longer, or at the end of the session as well. To work with the hooded eyes, you can use the following steps:

1. Close your eyes, just halfway. You should concentrate on trying to keep the eyelids from trembling in the process. While you spend this time concentrating on the eyelids, you are really working on relaxing the eyes a little bit, which can be super relaxing and helps with the strain that you may be feeling after speed reading for a bit.

2. Once you have gotten the eyelids to quit trembling, you can keep the eyes half closed, and gaze at some faraway object. You will notice that as you do this, your eyes are going to stop trembling a little bit.

Eye squeezes

This final exercise that we are going to take a look at to help improve the strength of our eyes is known as eye squeezes. This is another exercise that you can work with that are going to relax the muscles of the eyes, while also helping you to make these muscles more flexible, and can increase the amount of oxygen and blood that is able to flow to the eyes and the face. Not only does this help you improve your eye strength for easier speed reading, but it can also keep wrinkles away and make you look younger!

This exercise may take a little longer than what you will find with the other types of exercise, but it is still a good one to try out every once in a while, to ensure that you are working on your eyes and keeping them healthy and strong at the same time. Some of the things that you can do to help you get started on the eye squeeze exercise include:

1. As you inhale, going deep and slow, open your eyes and mouth as wide as you can. Work on stretching out each and every muscle in your face.
2. As you exhale, close and squeeze the eyes as tightly as you can. At the same time, you want to make sure that you are also squeezing in all of the muscles of the head, neck, and face. You should also clench the jaws a bit.
3. Hold the breath out for 30 seconds, making sure that you squeeze everything for that whole time. This may be hard in the beginning, but with some practice, you will be able to do it and really work on those muscles well.
4. Repeat the steps above another four times. If you need to, take a short break in between them. If you are able to do so, take another break and then do another set of five to really work on the muscles. If you can't do more, at least get through that original set of five to work on the muscles, and then work up from there.

Since this exercise usually takes a bit longer to work on and complete than some of the others, it doesn't need to be done each time, unless you are setting aside half an hour or more for your practice. But it is still a good one to work on, or implement, into your practice at least once a week. It provides so many benefits to your whole face and all of the muscles that you use while reading, especially when it comes to speed reading.

All of these great eye exercises are going to enhance what you are able to do with some of the other techniques that we discussed in this chapter. You should consider doing at least one or two at the beginning or the end of each speed reading session. This will ensure that you are able to get the best results out of the process and when your eyes get stronger, you will be able to skim and use the other techniques to their full potential.

When you are practicing your speed reading, you will need to do a bit of experimenting to find out which technique is going to work the best for you. Each person is going to work in a slightly different manner than others, so you will need to try out a few different kinds to ensure that you are able to get the one that works the best for you. And once you find the technique that clicks for you, your reading speed will increase in no time.

Chapter 5
WHERE PEOPLE GO WRONG WITH SPEED READING

Speed reading can be a very easy way for you to make sure that you can get through a lot of information in a short amount of time. There are a lot of great techniques that you are able to work with to help you increase your speed, and these will help you to get through a lot of material in a short amount of time, while also increasing your comprehension at the same time.

However, some mistakes can be made when it comes to working on speed reading. Learning how to avoid these mistakes can make a big difference in how successful you are with speed reading. Let's take a look at some of the ways that people may go wrong when they first get started with their own speed reading journey.

Common Mistakes with Speed Reading

Learning to do speed reading can be a huge time saver, and it can even help you to benefit your academic or professional career tremendously. However, if you are going through speed reading and you fall prey to some of the common reading mistakes, then you are going to miss out on some of the great benefits that come with it. Some of the most common mistakes that you can see when it comes to speed reading includes:

Reading through everything at the same speed

When you are first learning how to speed read, you may assume that you must read each and everything that you see at the same speed. This mistake can be hard to avoid because many readers are going to use their finger or hand to help guide their eyes. Because they do this, they will end up going line by line, staying at the same speed. This can sometimes seem like they fall into a rhythm, regardless of what they are reading.

Working this way doesn't make a lot of sense. Not everything that you read about is going to be equally important. You will quickly find that you can go through a document and find some sentences, and some paragraphs, that are going to be more important than the others. You can speed through some of the simple stuff and then slow down when it comes to some of the more important things.

There are a few ways that you can make sure that you are able to adjust your reading speed. This makes your reading more efficient to ensure that you are reading to get the most comprehension possible. Some of the things that you can do to adjust your speed include:

1. **Adjusting the speed to fit the type of material you are reading:** You should speed up on any of the material that is easier to get through, such as magazines, and then slow down the speaking a bit on material that may be a bit more technical, such as what is found in textbooks. This ensures that you can keep up with the material and understand what is going on no matter the situation. Besides, if you are already pretty familiar with the material and what is inside, you can push yourself to get through it faster.

2. **Adjust the speed to fit your purpose:** If the purpose of doing the reading is just to get to know the basics of content or material, then you don't need to slow down. Try to fly through that material as fast as possible. But if you need to go through and get a ton of details, then it wise to take a slower approach to reading.

One of the hardest decisions to make when you are trying to speed through a document is whether you need to speed up or slow down on that particular document. You will learn how to strike this balance a bit better as you get more practice with your speed reading.

Re-reading through unnecessary things

At some point or another, all of us have gone back and re-read some material. But there are many times when this is not necessary because you have gathered all of the information from the start anyway. You should never go back after you just get done with one sentence though. While it is possible that you might not have fully understood that sentence, it is also possible that the following one will clear things up. You may even need to finish out the paragraph to fully understand what is being said.

You don't want to waste your time going through and re-reading the whole paragraph or sentence each time. As you skim through and do the other reading techniques, you will quickly find that you are able to catch the majority of what is being said as long as you just keep going.

If you are prone to re-reading the things that are in your documents, then this is one of the first things that you need to work on fixing to see some results. To help with this, start out with a smaller document. Speed read through it with some of the techniques that we have talked about, and force yourself to read through the whole thing, without going back and trying to re-read it. You may find that just pushing yourself forward and not letting yourself look backward, perhaps with a piece of paper over the things you already read, and see just how much you are still able to comprehend at the end.

Poor Concentration

When trying to increase your reading speed, you must have a lot of good focus. Poor concentration can destroy the comprehension that you have, regardless of whether you read slowly or fast. The better your concentration, the faster you are able to read. And if you can concentrate well, you may also be able to reach a better comprehension of the material that you are reading. Two simple tips that you can follow to improve your focus includes:

1. **Read with your hand:** This is going to help you to focus you by guiding your eyes across the line. If you use a pacer, your hand, or a pen, you will notice that you will keep moving forward, without re-reading the information again. Using your hand to guide is one of the most basic ways to help improve your focus while reading.
2. **Eliminate the distractions:** There are some distractions around you that you can actually control. If you are trying to see if you can focus on the reading better, then it's probably a good idea to make sure that the phone is off. Do you have the urge to check your social media, email, or other texts on your phone when it is time to read? Then turn it all off to help you out. If you can think of any other distractions that can

keep you away from your reading, then try to avoid and keep clear when practicing your reading.

Myths with Speed Reading

When you first get started with speed reading, you may have some preconceived notions about what it all entails and what it means. It is common for a lot of people to have these notions as well. But sometimes, these are going to get in the way of you actually seeing success with your own endeavors. Some examples of common speed reading myths include the following:

1. **When you speed read, you don't enjoy reading as much as before.** Many find that when they speed read, they are more efficient as a reader, and then therefore they will get more pleasure and meaning out of the documents they read. In fact, many get started with speed reading and then develop a love of reading afterward.

2. **You won't do well with comprehending the material.** If you accurately do speed reading, you will find that you are able to comprehend the information just fine. For some people,

after practicing speed reading, their level of comprehension usually increases naturally. You will be able to read words in context and then derive more meaning from the words you have read.

3. **You skip words when you do speed reading.**
4. **You have to use a pointer as your pacer to speed read:** This is one of the methods that you can use to speed your reading up a bit. But it isn't always necessary. You can use another tool to help with this or use one of the other methods without relying on your finger or a pointer. That is the beauty of speed reading; you get the freedom with how you choose to do the whole process by picking the method that works the best for you.
5. **Speed reading is hard to do:** Many people assume you need to have special skills to get started with speed reading. They often will think that if they don't have enough reading speed or enough intelligence or something else along the way, that speed reading is something that they are not capable of doing. But anyone is able to work with speed reading. As long as

you are ready to put in some work, you are going to see some results with speed reading.

What If I'm Not Improving with Speed Reading?

If you have tried some of the techniques above, and you find that your speed reading just isn't improving as much as you would like, it may be time to change things up. Maybe you are setting your goals too high. It is a great thing to have high goals, ones that are going to challenge you a bit to reach them. But if you want to jump up 300 words a week for the next month, then you are probably putting too much pressure on yourself.

Instead of doing this, set out goals that are realistic and going to work well for you. Maybe try to improve your reading by 100 words a minute for each week for a month. Or find another goal that seems to work the best for you.

You may also find that the technique you are using can cause issues, the place where you are speed reading is too difficult to concentrate in (perhaps because of all the noise), or something else is distracting you and making it difficult to do the reading that you want. Take some time to take a step back and try to see what is causing the trouble or thing that mind be hindering your progress. This is often the best thing to do if your struggling to see any form of progression or improvement.

When and When Not to Use Speed Reading

There are a lot of times when working with speed reading can be a great option to go with. When you want to keep up with the news but don't have a lot of time to read through all the articles and publications, speed reading can be a great option. When you need to find just the information that you need for work or for a report, then speed reading can save you a lot of time because you can skim and see if the article or document is even worth your time. If you just need to glance through a report or another document to make sure that you understand the gist of everything, then speed reading can be helpful.

But there are sometimes when speed reading isn't going to be a good idea. This is mostly when you need to fully understand the document and what is inside, rather than just getting the basics of it. If you have a legal contract, a report from work, or another document that may have a lot of sensitive information in it, and you want to make sure you get all of the information, then you need to actually read through the whole thing rather than chunking or skimming. You still can use speed reading with this type of material, but you don't want to let it become the primary way you read in these situations.

Speed reading is not best used when reading literature either. There is often a lot more plot information, talking and more and speed reading through it can make it more difficult to understand what is going wrong. You can use some of the techniques here, such as reading the chapter headings and the back cover to get some information on what is going to happen next, but for the most part, you will have to read literature at a slower and steadier pace to keep up with everything.

Many great things come with speed reading in your life. But you have to know how to do it the right way. Jumping right in without any preparation or without any idea of how to do the process, or when is the right time to work on the speed reading can just lead you to failure. Avoid some of the common mistakes that are found above, and you will become a speed reading professional in no time.

Chapter 6

COMPREHENSION WHEN SPEED READING

When you get started with speed reading, you may be concerned about whether your comprehension is going to fail. You may have heard stories in the past about others who have tried out speed reading and struggled to make it work. Maybe, they realized that their comprehension got worse, and, that they just couldn't stop subvocalizing.

However, speed reading is not the enemy of comprehension. In fact, if you speed read correctly, you will be able to increase your speed while reading and still understand and comprehend the content being read at the same time. In many cases, your comprehension will get better than it was before. Let's look at some of the particulars of comprehension during speed reading and how you increase your comprehension to get the most out of speed reading.

How Speed Reading Affects Comprehension

Many people think that when your speed reading, your comprehension will go downhill. They think that you will just read too fast to catch what is going on around you and what is in the document. Therefore, there are a lot of people who recommend sticking with regular reading rather than trying speed reading.

If you don't work with speed reading in the right way, and you just try to race through the material without using any of the techniques that we discussed in this guidebook, then you will surely run into issues with comprehension. Too many people like just to pick up a few words to say they got a lot of words done a minute. Doing this cuts down your comprehension because you aren't taking in the important stuff, the stuff that can help them understand what is actually going on in the document.

If you use the right techniques and you focus on speed reading at the right pace based on your skills, then you will actually see that your comprehension will increase with this method. There are several reasons for this. First, when you have to focus on the words that are in front of you to go quickly, you are less likely to daydream and lose your focus on the material. Since you have laser sharp focus for the material, rather than reading slowly and hoping that your mind doesn't drift off.

Also, speed reading can help you with comprehension because you spend time looking for the material and the information that is actually important. With traditional reading, you will spend your time looking through a lot of information to find what you need. In fact, you may get so caught up in the information that is not needed, that you will often miss out on the important things. This is why, if you do speed reading the right way, you will be able to catch more information and understand more out of each document that you read.

Retaining More Information during Speed Reading

There is no question that learning how to read fast can benefit you in many different ways. Learning to read faster is an important skill, such as learning how to use a computer or different software programs based on your business. This means that you can learn, practice, and improve on your reading speed. But when you are working on your reading speed, it is also important that you learn how to retain more of the information as well. Some tips that you can use to help you to retain the information when speed reading include:

Avoid Subvocalization

Subvocalization is a process where you pronounce the words that you read silently in your head as you go. This is something that we do without even realizing it in many cases because this is how we learned how to read. But if you keep going with this process, your reading speed isn't going to get faster. This process is only going to hinder your reading speed and can even distract you from the meaning that is in the text.

Do you know whether you subvocalize or not? The next time that you pick up a document or something to read, take a moment to see if you seem to read the words out loud in your head. The more aware you become with this habit, the easier it can be to break it. Practice reading faster to make this process a lot harder to do, allowing you to gradually break the habit.

Preview the information you are going to read

It can be harder to comprehend what information is in the text if you have no idea what it is about when you start. Before you go through and read something new, especially if you have no idea what the topic is about and if you find it challenging, then you should review the document first. Take a look at any summaries, who wrote the article, why they wrote it, and what you think the text will have inside.

Tracking your progress

It is impossible to know if you are even making any progress if you don't know where you got started at. Before you start with any of the techniques that we talk about in this guidebook, make sure that you take a short reading and comprehension test, as we talked about before. This gives you a baseline, to see where your reading level is at the beginning.

From there, you will then get a better idea of the best ways to improve your reading over time. As you work through your own reading and working on improving your speed, you will then be able to compare where you are to where you were, allowing you to see the improvement.

Try not to do these tests too often though. You are working on developing this skill, it isn't something that is going to happen overnight. After about two weeks, then you can go back and use the same test to see if your speed and comprehension are getting better. Try to stick with the same test, so your results are consistent throughout the process.

Learn how to skip the small words

This process isn't quite the same as skimming, but it can be similar, and it really will speed up how quickly you are able to read. Words like "a, the, an, it" and so on don't add a ton to your comprehension and stopping to read them will just slow you down even more.

Don't believe that this works. Go and take out a paragraph and eliminate all of the words that are three letters or less. Then, go through and read through the paragraph. You may notice that it is quite a few of the words in the document. But as you go through and read the words that are left, you will find that you can still get the gist and the basics that come with the document.

Now you can move this over to the other things that you read. Try reading through a whole page, or more, and see if you can skip over some of the smaller words. Even if you haven't perfected the other methods, just skipping over the small words, the ones that don't mean that much, can help you see some results in how fast you can read.

Techniques to Help Comprehend Better through Speed Reading

Being able to speed read is a great skill to have. It can help you to improve and progress your personal and professional life. But being able to read quickly is not the only thing to consider when we work on this skill. You must also comprehend the material that you decide to read. Without this comprehension, you are just wasting your time reading. Some of the tips that you can use when it comes to comprehending the material when you are speed reading includes:

Make sure the distractions are gone

Distractions are going to be your worst enemy when it comes to trying to increase your reading speed. You need to learn what are the biggest distractions for you and how to avoid them to see the best results. For example, most people find that their phones can be a big distraction. If it goes off and makes any noise, such as from a text message, email, or someone calling, their attention will go straight from the task at hand and over to the phone. Turn the phone off and even consider leaving it in another room if you can't keep your focus.

If there is a computer in the room and your planning on practicing, it is time to turn it off and not let it distract you at all. The dings from social media, emails, and other things can easily take your attention away from the reading. Turn the computer off so you can't even see the stuff pop up.

When it is time to practice your speed reading, make sure that you go to a room that is devoid of distractions. Find one that has good lighting, a chair that is comfortable and no distractions. If you can, try to do it at a time when others are not at home to prevent further distractions. You want to be in an environment that allows you to focus just on the speed reading and nothing else.

Slow down just a Little

Yes, we have spent a lot of time in this guidebook talking about speed reading and learning how to increase your words per minute. But if you are reading fast and not comprehending anything that it says, then this speed reading process is not going to be very effective for you. You have to increase your speed realistically, going at a speed that makes the most sense for your skills, not killing yourself to get faster too soon.

You do not want to go from 200 words per minute to 1000 words per minute in a week or so. This may mean that you are taking in more words, but you are definitely not comprehending much, and not taking in what your reading. You have to set goals that are realistic for your needs and your own personal reading level. You will get to 1000 words eventually if you keep working and practicing. But you will not get there in just a few weeks.

If you notice that you are able to increase your words per minute, but you notice that your comprehension goes down or starts getting worse, then you may be jumping ahead too fast. Slow down a little, even just 50 words per minute, and you may find that this is a better level for you to concentrate and comprehend on the information. You can always increase later on with a bit more practice.

Make sure you are well-rested

If you are tired or drowsy, it is much harder for you to concentrate on the material in front of you. You are more likely to fall asleep and read sentences over and over again because you can't even keep your eyes open, much less concentrate on the words that are in front of you on the page.

It is best to pick a time of day that you are well rested and can feel renewed, so you can pay more attention. If you feel a bit tired, and like you may get over comfortable in your chair, you may feel yourself glazing over staring at words and not being able to focus. Try taking small breaks when reading, but try not too take too long; fifteen minutes is enough to refresh the body without wasting a lot of time. But if you are really tired it may be a good idea to give it a miss this time round.

Release the stress so you can focus

If you are feeling a lot of stress, then it is going to be hard to focus and concentrate on any document you need to look at, and this makes it even harder to get the comprehension that you need. All of us deal with stress on a daily basis. Our modern world is stressful with thinking about work, school, kids, and everything else that needs to go on and get done. But we are in control over how we manage that stress and we can choose what to do about it.

To release stress, there are many methods that you can choose to help with this. Some people find that going on a regular exercise plan can help them out. Getting in 30 minutes or more of some kind of physical activity, whether it is weight lifting, running, cardio or some form of stretching or yoga, can help you to release a lot of stress, and it is really good for your whole body. Even if you don't have a lot of health goals to reach, exercise can be a great way to help you out, as it can also help to clear the mind enabling your reading to improve.

Others may find that journaling is a better option for them to go with. They can spend even ten minutes at the beginning or the end of the day. This can be a good way to set yourself up for some good thoughts right away in the morning. Or you can use it to clear out your head from everything that might be bothering you, so you can get to sleep easier. The journal entries don't have to be too long, but just use it as a way to release some of the stress that you already feel during the day.

Some people find that working with yoga and meditation can also help. Both of these can help to clear out the mind and make it easier for you to relax in ways that may have been harder to do otherwise. It is sometimes hard to get started with meditation because your mind may not want to quiet down from all the thoughts you have and the feelings you experience. But over time, you will get better at it, and you will see that meditation can really benefit you.

Preparation

Sometimes, if you just prepare yourself when you get started, you will be able to see a better comprehension of the material you are working on. This doesn't have to take very long and considering it saves you a lot of time reading the document as a whole, it is definitely worth your time.

The first thing that you should consider doing is taking a look at any summary that comes with the information. You can look at the back cover, the synopsis, or any other summary that comes with this document. This helps you to get an idea beforehand of what is in the document to start with, and some of the main keywords that you are able to work with. It won't go in depth too much, but it can be a great way to give you a general idea of what to look for in the document.

You can also take the time to look at the headings in the document. Look at chapter headings and subheadings. These will pretty much give you an idea of what is in that section of the document before you even start reading. This way, you have a good idea of what to expect and can just search out the terms that are the most important to you as you speed read through it.

Picking out some main keywords that you want to look for in the document ahead of time can be helpful. By looking at the chapter headings and the summary of the document, you should already have a decent list of what you want to look for in keywords. Write these down and keep them nearby. Your eye will be instantly drawn to these words and the ones near them, and this can help you get through the information fast.

If you are just reading a chapter or two in a textbook, take some time to read through the introduction and summary that goes with each one. Most of the information that you need will be found there. You will find the most common topics and key takeaways, and you can search for those as your speed reading to enhance the amount of reading comprehension you have.

Eat something before you start

Focus is one of the main reasons that a lot of people struggle with doing well in speed reading. People will often have something on their mind causing them not to be able to concentrate at all. One of the things that is on peoples minds regular can be a hungry stomach.

When you are hungry, it is hard to concentrate on anything. Not being able to concentrate will effect your reading and comprehension greatly. Before you sit down and work on your speed reading exercises, take some time to eat a small snack or supper if it is that late in the day. You don't want to stuff yourself in this process, but having enough to make the stomach comfortable can help you do well with comprehending what you read. You can instead focus on the words you see in front of you, rather than the rumbling in your stomach.

While reading fast is important and is the main topic of this guide, you also want to make sure that you are actually understanding and comprehending the words you see. You don't have to catch every word, but if you do some speed reading exercises and aren't able to comprehend a single thing that you read on the page, then you need to make some adjustments. Speed reading should help improve your concentration, not hinder it, so make sure to work on some of the tips in this guidebook to see how it can help you with your reading comprehension.

Chapter 7
Subvocalization

One of the biggest obstacles to you seeing success with your speed reading is the process of subvocalization. This is known as auditory reassurance. It is when you read through something and then say the words, either by mouthing them or saying them in your head. Your talking speed is much slower than what your mind can process, and if you are limiting yourself to only being able to read as fast as the mind can say the words, then you are going to run into some trouble with increasing your reading speed.

When we were all originally taught how to read, we had to learn how to do it out loud. This allowed the teacher and others to hear if we were saying the words right, so they could help us more to improve and see better results. Then, once we were considered fluent enough, we were told to say the words in our heads as we worked through this. This may be a common way to teach people how to read, but it is the basics of why we say the words in our head when we read. And this is where the habit of subvocalization is going to originate. It is common for many people to continue on with this habit for the rest of their lives because that is just what they are used to.

While this may be the way that we are used to doing things, if we want to be able to increase our reading speeds, then it is time to minimize this habit as much as possible. It is not necessary to read out every word on a page in our heads just to get an understanding of what is there. Yes, when we were younger, this was a skill to learn and reading the words out loud was necessary to help you learn how to read. But it isn't necessary for you to do this now to extract the meaning of them. In fact, many adults can get the meaning out of these words just by seeing them.

There are many situations when you can read without saying the word in your head at all. You may already be doing it in some way or another in your own personal life. For example, any time that you see a stop sign, you just stop, without reading the words out in your head or out loud. You may read out the word "stop" in a sentence on a page, but for the stop sign, you do not read it out at all. This is the same kind of skill that we want to learn how to use when we read any kind of document.

If you are like other readers, you probably end up subvocalizing all, or at least most, of the words that you read in your head. But you won't always subvocalize everything that you read. An example of this is if you were reading something and came across the year "1788". You probably went through and said, "Seventeen eighty-eight." You are more likely to understand the year by just seeing the number. But if you saw a big number, like 304,003,543,100, then you wouldn't go through and subvocalize all of that.

With the second number, you know that it is a big one, and the understanding of that can come quickly, without you having to go through and subvocalize it. If you did try to subvocalize this, then you would end up spending a ton of time reading through this due to the length of it. You will still get the idea that it is a big number, no matter which way you've done it.

Reading isn't necessarily about the words that you read, but more about extracting ideas, absorbing the information, and getting the details. Individual words all on their own aren't going to mean all that much unless they are surrounded by other words. Being able to group the words together will help you to go faster when you read.

Many of the words that we look at are just there for grammatical purposes, and they don't necessarily add to the meaning of the sentence. These would be words like "the, an, a". They don't provide the same kind of meaning that you will get from other words, and learning how to skip over them and not subvocalize them, will ensure that you are able to read through a document faster and still get the right comprehension from it.

Think about it this way: if you spend your time saying each word out loud in your head, this basically means that you are only able to read as fast as you can talk. While some people can do this a bit faster than others, it still doesn't allow you to get up to the reading speeds that you can find with speed reading, which defeats the purpose of these exercises. If you have to go through and say all the words that you see in your head, then your limit will always be your talking speed, and you will never be able to get through it any faster.

The average reading speed for most people will be somewhere between 150 to 250 words each minute. This is going to be the exact same as for what their talking speed will be. Because most people use subvocalization and say the words in their head, which slows them down. You can test this out on yourself if you are curious. Try doing some reading for one minute normally, and then try to read it out loud for a minute. If you are like most people, you will find that you are going to be pretty similar in both methods.

If you did this exercise and you notice that your reading speed did go more than 50 words a minute faster than the talking speed, then this is a good sign. This means that you are on your way to being able to speed read, because your reading speed isn't held back by your talking speed. If your speeds are about the same, that's fine too. You will be able to work on it and see some improvements.

Subvocalization is one of the most important things that you can work on to help speed up your reading. But changing this habit is much easier said than done. Turning this voice in your head off can be hard. For most people, it is more about minimizing the habit rather than eliminating it completely.

An example of this may be the sentence "The girl tied her shoes." Instead of reading out all of the words there, you could just read "girl tied shoes." This gets the same meaning out of it but cuts down the words, so you can get through it faster. Your eyes will still see the words, so it's not like you are actually skipping them, but it ensures that you read through and subvocalize fewer of them, so you can go through the document much faster. Remembering that a lot of the words that are found in each document are not essential when it comes to the meaning of the content, even if they are essential to the grammar of the documents content. You will just be skipping a lot of what is not needed to get to the overall meaning.

Now that we have taken some time to talk about why subvocalization is bad for you and can slow down your reading speed, there are sometimes when saying the words, you see in your head can be helpful. For example, if the material that you want to tread through has really difficult or technical terminology or information that you are not familiar with, subvocalization can help you get through it a bit easier. In these kinds of situations, saying the words out loud or in your head can help you to understand it better, and can even help you to expand out your own vocabulary.

If you need to memorize something word for word, then working with subvocalization is a great thing as well. How do you think actors are able to remember their own lines for a part? If you did speed reading, you might get the general idea of what the words are saying, but you will never be able to memorize them all. Reading the words out loud can be useful when you are trying to memorize something word for word. But when you do your regular type of reading, you will rarely need to know the whole thing word for word. You just need to read to get the main details, ideas, and information from the document, and this is where speed reading can help.

To help you boost your reading speed, you need to figure out the method that works the best for you to minimize the subvocalization that you have by saying just a few words out of each line. This speeds you up, rather than letting your talking speed be your limit.

But how do you know if your habit of subvocalization is actually changing? If you were to do a test and you find that you are reading over 300 words, especially if you were at just 150 to 200, words per minute, then this is a sign that you have cut down on the number of words that you are saying in your reading because you can't talk that fast. If you find that your reading speed is over 400 words a minute, then you are making a lot of progress, and you have really limited the number of words that you are saying in your head.

Best Ways to Minimize Your Subvocalization

Now that we have spent some time talking about subvocalization and all it means, it is time to look at some of the tools that you can use to minimize the skill as much as possible. The more that you are able to minimize this issue, the easier speed reading will be. You can tell that you are successful when you do the tests and see that your reading speed is getting faster than your talking speed. Some of the things that you can do to minimize the subvocalization that is going on in your head include:

Use your hand as a guide while reading

This is one of the techniques that we talked about earlier, but it not only helps you keeps pace with reading, but it can help you to reduce the amount of subvocalization that is going on. Your hand can be a great way to help guide your eyes, so you have to move along and not read everything out. You will be able to use your hand, or a pointer or another tool, to guide your eyes. Through this process, since you are forcing yourself through a bit faster and your eyes will focus more on the words that are important.

Find ways to distract yourself

To help minimize this problem with your reading, you can find ways to distract yourself, so you are less likely to say the words in your head. How can you distract yourself during reading? One way is to consider chewing some gum when you read. This may seem a bit silly, but people find that when they chew gum while reading, it distracts them from saying the words in their head. It has also been proven to help concentration in visual memory tasks.

Another way that you can stop this problem in your head is to use another voice. Some people have success with counting from one to three when they are doing their speed reading. While you do this, focus somewhere at the beginning of the line at one, then the middle for two, and then the end of the line for three. Doing this is going to make it easier to fixate on three groups of words, rather than just looking at each word in the line. You get the choice of saying the numbers and counting out loud or in your head. Either way, you can distract yourself from saying the actual words you are reading. Over time this gets easier, and you will be able to read through the words without saying them in your head.

Listen to some music while you read

Listening to music when you read can help in two ways. First, it is going to minimize the amount of subvocalization that you will have going on during the reading session. And it can help you to increase the amount of concentration you have for the document.

You have to be careful with the type of music you decide to you because not all of them will be effective at helping you concentrate. Don't go with a type of music that has lyrics in it, or any that has a strong beat because these turn your concentration off. You should also avoid any music that may remind you of other things, for this can cause your focus to go off course as you remember all of those memories.

The best bet here is to listen to some music that is instrumental. Most people find that working with classical music can work best for them. It is a soft melody, no lyrics, no strong beat, and it can really help you concentrate, whether you are reading or doing other work during that time. Classical music, or other similar types of music, will help you to improve your concentration right away and can really minimize the subvocalization habit that you have.

Pushing Yourself

You may have to push yourself to read a bit faster instead of just hoping that it will work. Let's say that your normal reading speed is at 250 words per minute. You should try to push yourself to go a little faster as often as you can. You don't need to go crazy, maybe 300 to 350 words per minute if you started at around 250 words per minute. When you take the time to push yourself into saying more words at a faster rate than normal, you will be able to minimize the amount of subvocalization that is going on inside your head.

This happens because you have to improve your focus to get in the extra words. You don't have to go crazy, but just sitting down and trying to push for that little extra speed, can make a world of difference.

There are a lot of different tools out there that you can use to help increase your reading speed. Some of the tools may make exaggerated claims that don't make sense and will be over the top for what you can actually do. But if you add in a lot more practice, and you take care in actually using the right tools, you are going to see some amazing results with how much faster you are able to read.

Chapter 8

Practice Makes Perfect

You are never going to see good results with speed reading if you don't take the time to practice the work and some of the techniques that we have talked about in this guide. It is important to get on a consistent schedule when it comes to working with speed reading. If you can do that, and learn how to push yourself, you will be amazed at how fast your reading speed can improve.

The first thing that you should consider is the best time to do your speed reading and how to practice. If you only practice once a week, or you find that you can only practice here and there, then this is a skill that will falter. Just like with any other skill you choose to obtain, you need to give your speed reading some practice to get better at it. Ideally, try spending at least a little bit of time practicing it each day if you can.

This doesn't mean that you have to spend hours on end practicing your speed reading to get better. In fact, practicing for this long is going to give you a headache and make it impossible to progress any further. You are exercising your brain with this skill, and spending too long on it can make things more difficult to comprehend and stick with. Short sessions, even just fifteen minutes, each day can make a slight difference in the results that you can see.

So, the first step here is to pick a time each day when you can focus on your speed reading endeavors. Schedule it like you would any other important meeting that you need to get done during the week. It only takes about fifteen to twenty minutes, but bringing out your planner and actually writing it down like an important appointment will make it more likely that you will follow and stick with it.

Maybe you find that working on it in the morning, right when you wake up, before the kids get up, is a perfect time. Maybe spending a few minutes during the day when you are on break, or in the evening when things have settled down. You can pick any time that works for you, just make sure that you can maintain your consistency and that you stick with it to enhance this skill.

Another thing that you need to consider is the spot where you would like to do your speed reading. You need to make sure that you find a spot that will enhance rather than hinder your reading and everything that you try to do. You need to find a place that is quiet and free of distractions. So, picking to do this in a loud office or in a coffee shop is not going to be the best idea.

If you have your own spots in your home, such as a bedroom or a small office, then this may an ideal place to read. Make sure that the computer is turned off, the phone is left somewhere else, and you can fully concentrate on the task at hand. If others live in the home with you, try to find some way to occupy them away from you for to ensure you can fully concentrate on the task at hand, rather than being interrupted the whole time.

Ok, so now that we understand that practice is so important to helping you hone your own skills with speed reading, it is important to be prepared when it comes to starting your practice sessions. The first thing to consider here is that you want to sit with comfort.

You don't want to pick out a chair that is so comfortable that you will fall asleep in it. But you also don't want to go through and have a chair that is so uncomfortable that you end up spending all of your time thinking about the chair rather than the reading at hand. A good office chair can be a good place to start so that you are comfortable but can still concentrate on the reading that you need to do.

The next thing to consider is how relaxed you are. You don't need to spend time getting so relaxed that you will fall asleep. But if you are angry or stressed out or some other issue that makes your body very uncomfortable and unrelaxed, then you are going to have a lot of trouble with concentration. If you aren't feeling the best or feel overwhelmed or have some other reason that you just can't seem to relax, then it is time to make some changes and figure out how to relax ahead of time.

There are many ways that you can make sure that you relax your body before you get started with speed reading. You can make sure that you have something to eat so you don't feel too hungry. You can take a warm bath to relax. Yoga and meditation can be great ways to relax the mind, get the brain to slow down a bit so you can concentrate on the reading instead of whatever problem is bothering you at the moment.

When you are ready to get started with your speed reading, it is time to prepare your mind to help you in your practice reading sessions. You can have your own routine, but there needs to be something that helps you go from the task that you were in before, to transitioning to the right frame of mind before you start. One method to use is to grab the material that you want to use, close your eyes, and then take three deep breaths before you get started. This can often be enough of a transition to help you feel focused and prepare for the reading for better results.

If you still need a little bit more of a transition to see results, then you may think about what you are doing a bit. After the deep breaths, consider telling yourself that you need to read with a purpose. You aren't sitting down to read with the idea of pleasure or even for business. You are doing it to hone this new skill, so take some time to work on it, rather than just trying to get it done and over with. When you know your purpose from the beginning, it is easier to train the mind to get the results that you want, and your reading speed will instantly improve.

There are a lot of different things that you can choose to read through when you practice your speed reading. You can choose to read things like a magazine article, newspapers, books, documents, emails, and more. You can choose to speed read anything that you would like. One option that works well is to practice with the help of newspaper columns.

Newspaper columns are usually really easy for you to speed read through. Many times, the first few paragraphs are going to have all the information that you need. If you spend just a few minutes or less reading those first few paragraphs, you will get all of the information that is needed in order to take in the article information. Then the rest of the newspaper article is going to contain a few more details, but you can use the information from the beginning to get through it all with just skimming and taking a look at. You won't find anything new or exciting through the end of the article, so it can be skipped, or just skimmed to get the rest of the information that you need. Plus, newspaper columns are really fast reading anyway and you probably already skim through them anyway, so it is a great way to practice.

Of course, you don't have to work with newspaper articles to practice your speed reading. You can choose other options as well based on what you are interested in. It is best to speed read with something that is nonfiction. The way that fiction is set up is a bit different, and is not ideal for speed reading. Working with a nonfiction book is a much better way to ensure that you are working on something that is effective with this skill.

With that in mind, remember that you can choose any kind of nonfiction work that you would like. Think about something that greatly interests you, and then pick out some books that are on this topic. This way, you can enjoy the information that you are reading and can learn something at the same time. Just because you are working on a new skill doesn't mean that you can't have some fun and enjoy what you are doing during the process.

Skimming is another thing that you should work on during your practicing time. We have spent some time talking about skimming and how it can be useful for the speed reading process. With this, practice searching for sentences that are on the page that may have the main idea that should be in the document. You should learn how to do this in a manner that allows you to skip over text that is just filler, that is less interesting, and information that is not as relevant as it could be to the main idea. This can be useful in so many aspects of your life, and being able to increase your speed with skimming can ensure you get all the main parts of the document, without having to waste time with all the extra stuff.

When you work on speed reading, you need to make sure that you are practicing all of the different techniques that we talked about before. Many of them can be effective and can help you get faster, but one of the best options is to learn how to guide your reading with a pointer or your finger. This is one of the most effective methods for speeding up your reading, and if you haven't tried it out, you should give it a chance for at least one practice session. This is something that will help greatly if you run into any problems while trying to speed read.

The method is so simple - you just use a finger or some kind of pointer, like a pen, to help guide the eyes. You can use this pointer to decide how fast you should be reading at. If you want to slow down, move the pointer at a slower speed. If you want to move faster, then you move the pointer a bit faster. You don't have to limit yourself to making movements across the page just going left to right.

Sometimes, you can increase the reading speed even more if you move the pointer in different shapes across the page. Using a finger or a pen to make some of these shapes on the page can help speed up the visual cortex, allowing your visual span to increase, so you learn how to take in a whole line at a time rather than just one or two word. It also makes it easier to imprint the information that you read to the subconscious mind to look at later. It also can help with subvocalization, so it is definitely something to consider when you are working on your speed reading.

Another thing that you may want to work on is how to use the skills and tools of the brain more effectively so that it can go through and read faster. There are already some maps that exist inside the brain that help you to recognize words and understand what is going on around you. If you are able to get these to be more efficient, you will find that it is easier to move through the familiar concepts and words that you see on the page at a much faster rate than before.

If you ever come up against some content that is a bit unfamiliar to you, then make sure that you give it its proper due and really learn it. This helps you to form those strong maps in the brain a bit better. The more that you learn these topics, the easier it is for you to prove the information quickly later on. It will then get imprinted on the brain, and the next time that you read about it, you can skim through it and speed read through it without any problems at all.

You can also practice some of the different things that we discussed in this guidebook in your daily life, even when it isn't one of your regular practice sessions. For example, the next time that you see a signboard outside of a restaurant or another store in your area, glance at it and then look away. Were you able to recall what was on it? If you are just starting with speed reading, you probably can't read through it very well. But after some practice, you will be able to do this with just a glance at anything, and reading a sign with a glance and comprehending what is on it will seem like nothing at all.

Some of the other things that you should consider trying out when it is time to work on your speed reading include:

- ❖ **Keep the harmful distractions out of the way:** Reading faster is always about maximizing your concentration as much as possible. So, make sure that you are able to support this goal. Keep the designated area free of any noisy electronic devices, like your video games, your television, your computer, your phone, or anything else that could keep your mind away from what you want to accomplish. If the area already functions as a study space, then this should already be set up well for you. But you can use any room that you want for this process, just make sure that you hide away anything that is going to cause distractions and issues for you.
- ❖ **Learn how to eliminate the problem with regression:** Regression is basically the process of re-reading the same passages over again.

Doing this even just once during the session can slow you down a lot. This is often due to lack of concentration, but many different issues can come into play here. You need to learn how to stop this to increase your speed. Working in three to four-word clusters of words, working with skimming, and using something that blocks the passages you have read, such as a piece of paper, so you are forced to move forward and not go backward can be something that works well.

❖ **Increase your eye movements:** There are several exercises that you can work with that will boost your eye movements, and can make it easier to read faster. One method that you can work on is to read a first paragraph or passage at a normal speed for a minute. Then read it three additional times, but have your index finger move you along the page. Double and triple your reading speeds each time you do this. During the additional times, focus on some of the keywords to help you with comprehension as well. This can help you to move the rate at which your eyes read the words, and can help in so many ways later on when it comes to your reading speed.

❖ **Figure out ways to minimize the amount of subvocalization**: This is the single biggest thing that is going to cause you to slow down with your reading speed. You need to learn how to turn this off, or you are always going to be limited to your talking speed when it comes to your reading speed. We have discussed a lot of ways that you can limit your subvocalization, but during your practice sessions, make sure that you try out a few of these as well.

❖ **Vary your reading speeds:** Before you get started, you should consider the different intellectual demands of any kind of material that you choose to read. You can then adjust the speed to match. If you are reading an entertainment article for fun, you can definitely read through it much faster than reading on a topic about programming. A good reader is able to figure out the overall complexity of the information, and then they determine how much time they need to spend on the content. Sometimes they are able to skim over it, and other times they know they need to spend more time on it to get the information that they need.

Setting some time aside to help you learn how to speed read can be so important to ensure that you see the results that you want. You are never going to get better with your reading if you just work on it occasionally or you never work with it at all. Use the tips in this chapter to set up a good time and routine for practicing that you can maintain and stick with on a consistent basis, and you will find that your reading speed will increase in no time at all.

Chapter 9
Speed Reading Studies

This guide has spent a lot of time talking about speed reading and why it can be so great for your overall professional and personal life. We have shown that there are a lot of benefits that come with speed reading, and being able to read through things much faster can be really helpful when it comes to getting through documents and other literature as quickly as possible. But how much truth is there when it comes to speed reading? Is this actually something that works? Are you actually able to learn how to read quickly and go from about 200 words per minute to over 1000 words per minute? This chapter is going to take a look at, and shed some light on some of the studies for speed reading

Be Careful with Sites that Try to Sell You Speed Reading Programs

There are a lot of people who want to be able to learn how to speed read, and also be able to learn to do it in a short period of time. They want to receive all of the benefits that come with speed reading without having to spend weeks doing it. Because of the increased interest in speed reading, there are a lot of companies out there who will make big promises, like getting you to increase your word count in no time at all, often with time limits that don't make sense compared to the level you are at.

These companies will state that they can help you increase your reading speed in just a few weeks, taking you from 200 words to 500 words in that time, and then to an even higher level straight afterwards. This may sound like a great deal, but honestly, this is way more than what most people can do, and the amount that they charge you is going to be outrageous. Considering that you can increase your reading speed with your finger and some reading material that you find online, there is no reason that you should spend hundreds of dollars letting someone else "tell" you how to do it.

Learning the basics of speed reading may seem like one of the best strategies for making quick work of reports, emails, and other texts that we need to encounter each day. But there has now been a comprehensive review of the science that is behind reading, and it shows that the claims that are put out there by quite a few reading programs and tools are often too good to be true. This review took time to look over the research that was done over a decade about the science of reading. Through this, a team of psychological scientists found that there is little evidence that speed reading is a shortcut to understanding and remembering larger volumes of written content in a short amount of time.

The scientists state that the training courses for speed reading have been around for a long period, and they have found that there is a recent surge in how many technologies are now available for speed reading. The point of the study was to take a closer look at the science that is behind reading and look to see whether or not the technologies and the paid programs were actually able to increase speed reading and if this could benefit your comprehension. According to Elizabeth Schotter, a psychological scientist at the University of California, San Diego, "We wanted to take a close look at the science behind reading to help people make informed decisions about whether to believe the claims put forth by companies promoting speed reading technologies and training courses." This is the reason that the review was done in the first place.

This particular report was published by Psychological Science in the Public Interest to take a look at how great speed reading works and if it can benefit you. This study found that speed reading could be beneficial to helping you get through larger amounts of text quickly, and when it is used properly, you will be able also to comprehend the information better. But, many of the techniques that are used by the big companies trying to sell their products and technologies make promises that just aren't realistic, and most people are disappointed and frustrated by the results that they get.

Reading is considered a complex dance with a few different visual and mental processes, and researchers have found that many skilled readers are already reading through things pretty quickly on their own, averaging between 200 and 400 words per minute. But there are some speed reading technologies will make claims that say that those who use their technologies will be able to boost the speed seven times more because they are able to eliminate the need to make eye movements by presenting the user with words quickly on the phone or computer screen.

The issue with this is that the eye movements that you use are only going to account for about ten percent of the time, overall, that you spend reading. By eliminating the ability to go back and reread previous words and sentences tends to make comprehension worse, rather than better in many cases. The biggest obstacle with how fast we can read, according to science, isn't really in our vision and our eye movements, but in how well we are able to recognize the words on the page, and the processes that we use to combine those words to make meaningful sentences.

However, even though the speed reading technologies are not going to really be able to help you increase the speed that you are able to read at, you will find that skimming can be a really effective method to help you out. In fact, research has found that the people who are the most effective at speed reading are actually effective at skimming. This can be even more effective when you have a little bit of understanding and familiarity with the topic at hand, which means that they are able to find the right keywords and get through the information a bit faster.

Another thing that can help with boosting how well you are able to read through a topic is practicing your reading for comprehension. Greater exposure to writing, no matter what kind of form it is in, can help you to have a larger and richer vocabulary. It can also help you learn more contextual experience that is going to help you to anticipate upcoming words based on what you are already reading, so you can then get through the material faster.

No matter what, it is healthy to have a bit of skepticism when it comes to speed reading and what may or may not work for you. There are a lot of programs out there that claim they can increase your reading speed in no time. Some of them may be able to help. But you can also work with increasing your speed reading all on your own without the help of other tools, and without having to pay out a lot of money to get it done either. Always being a skeptic and picking out the program that works the best for your needs is the best option to go with.

Additional Studies about Speed Reading

There have been numerous studies done on speed reading and whether or not it is an effective tool in helping you to comprehend more and see the best results with getting things done. One study shows that the maximum that we can read, without skipping any of the words that are on the page, is about 500 words a minute. This assumes that there is no backtracking either, although about fifteen percent of the time that we spend reading is going to be for regressions. It also assumes that there isn't much comprehension beyond identifying the words. But in practice, studies have shown that most of us are going to be able to read around 250 words a minute.

Of course, remember that with most of the methods of speed reading that we do, we aren't going to spend our time reading each and every word. Most of the words on the page are there for grammatical reasons, rather than for the meaning or for comprehension. So, we can already speed up beyond that 500 words just by figuring out which words aren't necessary and learning how to skip them.

Another study that we need to look at is one that shows that reading faster than 500 words can be possible. However, a lot of these studies need to change up the way they conduct the survey and the research that bring them more into the mainstream. For example, one of these studies found that after participants spend 16 hours doing training for speed reading, they would be able to read at a significantly faster speed than before. This shows that speed training can be effective; however, there weren't any control groups in the study, so it is possible the participants were just able to become familiarized with the experimental procedure from one test to the other, or they had reading materials that were a bit easier the second time they did the test.

Other studies are also going to boast impressive improvements, but they are going to rely on a device that is known as a tachistoscope. What this is, is a tool that is going to flash the words on a screen for briefer and briefer periods of time until the person is able to read through them very quickly, but this isn't the same as being actually able to read through the material. Without this tool, the readers found that it was difficult to go back to regular reading and see results, making it very ineffective.

About ten years ago, Keith Rayner, a psychologist and one of the most widely respected experts in the field on what the eyes are doing when we read, was able to pinpoint one single study of speed reading as both rigorous and interpretable. Inside of this study, psychologists spent time monitoring how the eyes moved for speed readers, or readers who were able to take in 600 to 700 words per minute, and the eye movements of those who were considered normal readers, or who could read 250 words a minute.

In this study, the researchers determined that those who were speed readers were able to move their eyes more quickly because they didn't make as many fixations as the other readers did. Instead of reading through each and every word that was in the document, they were able to read a few words here and there.

Another interesting thing about this study is that the researchers tested those who did speed reading and found that these readers did pretty well on general questions, just from the basics that they read through the document and some of the pre-existing knowledge that they had on the document itself. But when they were tested on the little details of the text, they missed out and often did poorly here.

This is close to what we already know happens with speed reading. This is meant to give you the basis of a topic and can help you with some conversation starters or getting things done with the information, but you aren't going to be able to list off a ton of details about it. If you need to read through a document and get all the information out of it, or you know it is a technical or new topic, then you will need to slow down, as we have already discussed earlier.

We also took a look at how your eye fixations need to be limited when you speed read. This helps you to make fewer stops when you are reading, and it can help you to see faster results than usual. This is what was seen in the study. Speed readers were able to go through the text at a much faster rate because they didn't stop at each and every word like normal readers would do.

In this same study, the researchers asked the normal readers to skim the text and see if they were able to get to 600 to 700 words a minute. These skimmers eye movements and their results on comprehension tests ended up being about the same as the speed readers.

This shows that you definitely don't need to spend a ton of money on a speed reading seminar to get results. You just need to be able to read through and skim the text, with a bit of practice of your own, to increase your reading speed.

What is really amazing out of this is that it is believed that some people are able to read up to 2500 words a minute, but none of them have been tested yet to see how this works and how their comprehension is during this. These individuals may be a little above what most of us can do and perhaps have more of a photographic memory, where they are able to just glance at the page and remember everything that is on it. Since most of us are not able to have this skill and a photographic memory isn't something that you can gain with practice, it is something that you are born with, we may just have to deal with the slower reading speeds and work on seeing if we can make them a little faster to help us out.

Knowing When to Slow Down

Now, there are many different reasons why you would want to learn to speed read. It can make reading more enjoyable because no one wants to spend hours trying to get through even the most basic of topics. You will find that it helps you get your work done because you are able to actually get through it all and move on, rather than just concentrating on the reading. It can help you when you speak to others and when you need to communicate with them better because you have the right information to converse and not feel nervous along the way.

Even with all of the good things that come with speed reading, experts and studies alike will bring up the point that it is a good idea to learn when its best to slow down on things. Speed reading can be done with a wide variety of materials. You will find that it works well with newspaper articles, magazines, some nonfiction books, and other materials that you may already have some familiarity with. But for those brand new topics or the ones that are more technical and harder to work with, you will find that it may be better to slow down a bit.

This isn't to discourage you from reading fast and seeing how much you can build up this skill. But your comprehension will struggle in some cases. Speed reading isn't always the biggest problem with this because with regular reading your focus is going to drift off and comprehension can go down, while this is less likely to happen when you are speed reading. But still, you will find that comprehension can often lack when you are working on a more complex subject.

What this means is if you are working on some sort of tough or complex material, go ahead and slow down. If you are studying for a psychology test and you know nothing about psychology, then slow down. If you are learning a new language and trying to figure out some of the rules that go with it, then slow down when reading. Any time that the subject may seem a little bit difficult for you to handle, or you don't understand how it works at all, then take a slower approach to reading it.

This doesn't mean that you can't use some of the techniques that we have talked about in this guide to help you read faster. These can still be utilized and will ensure that you are able to get through the material faster than normal. But, you should slow down and not try to speed through things when you are first learning them or if you find them difficult at all.

Speed reading has captured the attention of a lot of people over the years. Many people are interested in learning how to master speed reading to improve many different aspects of their life, both professionally and personally. Whether you want to use it to help improve your communication skills with others or because you want to speed through the work that needs to be done, working with speed reading can be a great way to get started.

Conclusion

Thanks for making it through to the end of this book. Let's hope it was informative and able to provide you with all of the tools you need to achieve your goals whatever they may be.

The next step is to put some of these techniques into practice and see how it can work for you. While many think that speed reading can be a difficult thing to work on, it is actually pretty easy and fun. You just need to make sure that you pick a technique that you find effective, and then maintain some steady practice with it. But don't be shy when it comes to trying different techniques, some may be for you and some may not.

This guide has took some time to discuss the different ways that you can get started with speed reading in your own life. We have looked at the benefits of speed reading, some of the techniques that you can use, how to stop the problem of subvocalization, and how to increase your comprehension at the same time. When you put all of these lessons into practice you will be able to increase your reading speed and see some amazing results.

It may take some time for you to find your edge, but eventually you will get there, and you will be speed reading like a pro

The Unknown Methods of Critical Thinking

By Dale Owen.

Introduction

The following chapters will discuss everything that you need to know about critical thinking, and how it can be used to benefit your life in so many ways. Critical Thinking is used to help give us a good idea of how and what decisions we should make, especially when our emotions get the better of us. It can also help you to become a better person and form better relationships with those around you.

In this guide we will take some time to discuss the various elements of critical thinking. We will talk about the ways in which you can benefit from critical thinking, how to go through the different stages and steps to becoming a critical thinker, and how to ask the right questions to help you solve various problems.

We will also spend a little time talking about problem-solving and decision-making. Both of these are very important aspects when it comes to critical thinking and understanding how they work, how they can be of benefit, and how they can improve the way you think.

There are plenty of books on the market about this subject, so thanks for choosing this one! Every effort was made to ensure it is full of as much useful information as possible, and easy to follow.

The only thing I ask is if you could please leave an honest review upon finishing the book, thanks

Chapter 1
Understanding Critical Thinking

There are many things that we often need to think about and make decisions about on a daily basis. Some of these things consist of: what to eat, when to get out of bed, whether we want to try something new, what to get at the store, how fast to drive, whom to hang out with, and so much more. Some of these decisions don't sound of much importance but they can often be the things that can change the course of our whole day or even our whole lives.

Learning how to be a critical thinker can make a big difference in your life. It allows you to look at all of the possible solutions with the information and facts that you have researched. Once you've mastered using your brain's ability to think, you will find that it is easier to make harder decisions a lot quicker. Let's take a look at some of the basics that you need to know to understand how critical thinking works and what it can mean.

What Is Critical Thinking?

Critical thinking is basically the ability for you to apply reasoning and logic to new or unfamiliar ideas, opinions, and situations. When we learn how to think critically, it means that we can see things in a more open-minded way, and that we will take the time to look at all concepts and ideas from as many angles as possible. While we may not even realize it, critical thinking is an important skill that helps you to take a look past your own views of the world so you can get a better understanding of why people think in certain ways. You may find that you will use it often when you are in a debate so you can form better arguments for your side.

The ability of thinking in a critical way is essential. It helps you to create new possibilities when it comes to problem-solving. While there are a lot of people who are against critical thinking, it is actually a method that allows you to be more open-minded because you have to seek out different answers to a current problem you are working with. You also need to be willing to accept an answer, even if it isn't the one that you were planning on hearing.

Open-minded thinking requires that someone is not going to assume that their own approach is the right way or the best way. They have to be willing to take different steps or a different course of action no matter what it is. For example, if you were a scientist, you would need to be open to the idea that when you do an experiment, you will always have to be open to a result that you probably were not expecting

Being open minded will allow it to be much easier for you to find out new things and discover more than before. You won't be limited by the limiting beliefs you had going into it to start with. This can be a challenge in some cases, but you will find that it provides you with tremendous and meaningful discoveries that you would have missed out on in the past.

Another part of critical thinking that you need to pay attention to is the ability of the person to approach any situation or problem rationally. Being rational requires that you analyze all of the information that you know. From there, you can make analyses and judgments based on evidence, rather than on your own emotions and opinions.

An honest approach to reasoning means that the critical thinker needs to acknowledge their own emotions, motives, and personal goals and realize that these are going to have some influence on your opinions and on the way that you think about things. Rational thought can sometimes involve finding and then getting rid of any prejudices that you already have. This helps you to be objective and can bring a fresh approach to any problem that you may encounter.

In many cases, critical thinking is going to rely on your ability to take a look at the world in a way that won't focus on your personal self. This can be something that doesn't come easy to most. We are already in our own minds, having emotions, thoughts, and experiences that can color the way that we see things. But we end up letting these things color our own experiences and the way we feel about things determine the decisions that we make day to day.

Being able to empathize with a person means that the thinker must be able to stop thinking about themselves for a short amount of time, and instead put themselves in the place of someone else. This can help you to learn cooperation, teamwork, and communication skills when you use more empathy. This is why empathy, as well as critical thinking skills, are so valuable in many professional fields.

So, how do we use this? An effective critical thinker, to begin with, is a thinker who takes the time to analyze what they know about the subject. They will need to make the extra effort to recognize what they don't know about a topic. This can form an initial knowledge base for consideration. The thinker can take some time to look at what research is out there about the subject. It is their job to identify what they can learn, just by looking over all of the research that is out there.

Often the skills that you need to develop to be a critical thinker are the same as what you can find in science. A scientist can take a close look at what they see in the world, makes a prediction (while still keeping themselves open-minded enough to accept answers that may be different from that prediction), and then they go through and try to find all the information to either prove or disprove your theory in the end.

When you try to take this approach in your own personal life, you will learn how to place more emphasis on finding the preconceived notions and prejudices that you already hold. This allows you to work in eliminating and even avoiding these opinions so that you can come up with a more objective or honest review of any issues. This can be applied in many different scenarios that you encounter.

Having the ability to think in this manner can help you out in so many ways. You can actually think things through properly. You will take a look at all the facts and make an informed decision. You refuse to allow your prejudices, and your emotions take over and make the decisions for you. This helps you to make the best decisions for your needs and can make it easier for you to form lasting and healthy relationships in your personal and professional life.

Critical thinking can be used in many different ways. Students may use it to evaluate the plot of a book or when they want to figure out the motives of a character in a literature class. Someone on the debate team would have to spend time thinking about a subject in a critical manner to form up a strong argument and anticipate all of the points that their competitors would try to make. Many people are going to use empathy and open-mindedness in their personal lives to help them get tasks done as effectively as possible and to make it easier to work as a team.

Critical thinking can be used in many different areas of your life. Learning how to use it on any situation that you encounter can make a big difference in how you approach a situation, how you get along with others, and so much more.

What Are the Critical Thinking Skills?

There are a lot of different skills that you need to have when you want to work on your critical thinking skills. Let's take a look at the top seven critical thinking skills that you can work on:

1. **Analyzing:** This is when you will need to take the information that you receive, break it up or separate it into parts so that you can discover what the true nature, functions, and relationships are all about.
2. **Applying the standards:** This is when you are going to take the information that you received and then choose to judge on it according to rules and criteria that are already established.

3. **Discriminating:** This is when you can take the time to recognize the similarities and differences among situations and other things. Then, you can take each one and give them a category or a rank based on what they fit in the most with.
4. **Information seeking:** This is when the individual will take his or her time to search for evidence, facts, or knowledge. This can be done by looking for relevant sources and gathering the best data from the sources that you have.
5. **Logical reasoning:** This is when you will need to draw some conclusions or references that are supported with the help of the evidence that you found.
6. **Predicting:** This is when you envision a plan and some of the consequences that may come with it before making your final decision about it.
7. **Transforming the knowledge:** This is when you will convert or change the condition, nature, form, or function of concepts for different contexts.

What Critical Thinking Involves

To start, critical thinking is going to involve a lot of logic, but when we look at the definition, we are looking more at truth compared to logic. Critical thinking involves a sort of reflection on what we are being presented in terms of information. We get to look at that information and decide whether we should accept that as a valuable idea, an action, or behavior, rather than letting others tell us what to think. We can look at the situation objectively, regardless of our current moods or who presented the information to us in the first place.

For example, you may decide to watch television late at night. During this time, you may see a lot of commercials for various food joints around town. When we stop to ask ourselves whether it is a good idea to go out and pick up some junk food early in the morning or not show that we are using this kind of thinking. We may take some time to draw up reasons why we should and shouldn't do it, leading us to weigh out both sides and make a decision.

It is important to remember that just because we are using critical thinking doesn't mean that we will always make the right decisions. Sometimes, we try to use this critical thinking and then we come up with the wrong or maybe just a bad conclusion. We will need to do the math to help us figure out if we are reaching the right answer.

Now, there is also a thing known as non-critical thinking. This is a bit different than you may think when you look at the other options. To start, non-critical thinking is just the absence of being engaged in the process of critical thinking, but it doesn't necessarily mean that you are being dumb or irrational.

We may spend more time working with non-critical thinking on a regular basis because it is easier to do. If you never think critically, then this is going to cause some issues, and you may miss out on a lot of opportunities. But, sometimes, such as when you are listening to music or playing a little game with someone else, the non-critical thinking or thinking that doesn't mean you to use analysis to can come up with the solutions that you need.

Qualities and Characteristics of Critical Thinkers

Critical thinkers view the world in a different way than most of us are used to. They will take a look at a situation or any decision that they are faced with, and take the time to consider all of the different options before they make that final decision. They will solve a problem in a manner that provides the best results, not the solution that has always been used.

But what are some of the most common characteristics found in someone who is considered a critical thinker? There are a number of traits that you will find in these individuals, and some of the characteristics may surprise you a little. Let's take a look into some of these traits, and the things that you can even work on to help you to improve your thinking game.

The first trait is curiosity. Those who are critical thinkers are very curious about a lot of different topics, and they often will have a very broad interest. If you find that only few things interest you, and you don't like to look up or research into things, then you may need to work on your critical thinking skills. Critical thinkers tend to have a healthy amount of inquisitiveness about the world and even about other people. They may even have an appreciation for and an understanding of the diversity of beliefs, cultures, and views found in the world, even if they vary from their own. This is one of the reasons that they are great lifelong learners.

They are also known to have compassion. While critical thinkers are often mistaken as people who have no feelings and who don't empathize well with others, this couldn't be farther from the truth. Many times, these thinkers act just as much with their hearts as they do with their minds. They understand that the world is already full of a ton of segregation and judgment; you can't do much without having someone nearby who is ready to judge on how you do it. More than often, these negative things are going to happen due to a lack of understanding of how each person approaches a problem.

For example, someone from a different part of the world may have a different worldview than you. Someone from the city may have a different viewpoint compared to someone from the country. Someone with two parents at home will see things differently than someone who has just one parent at home. Each of us have our own story that makes us who we are. We all also have our own challenges and trials that have worked to shape and make us a unique individual. People who can think critically can recognize these different histories, and they will compassionately celebrate all of the uniqueness found in everyone. They can also see the best in themselves and in others.

Next, we need to take a look at the characteristic of awareness. Opportunities to apply your skills in critical thinking present themselves all the time. Effective critical thinkers will remain tuned into this fact, and they will keep themselves on high alert for any chance that is needed to apply the very best thinking habits no matter what situation they are in.

You will find that the best critical thinkers do not take anything they hear or see at face value. These are the people who will keep on asking questions, and they will continue to explore each and every side of an issue to find the right decision. This makes many of them instinctual problem solvers simply because they are aware that they need to always research and figure out the right answer for themselves.

Decisiveness can be a great trait for many critical thinkers as well. A lot of decisions need to be made quickly throughout your life. When you are a critical thinker, you can take the time to weigh out all of the options and then imagine the outcomes right then and there, with lots of clarity and speed, without wasting time. There are many instances where regular thinkers will take too long to make a decision, this will often cause them to miss out on something.

There are even some situations where we must make our own decisions, even if the information we need isn't there. When you face any kind of challenges, there is a chance that someone will need to take the lead, leading them having to make some hard decisions, ones that many others will shy away from. Many times, the critical thinker realizes that, sometimes, it is necessary for them to take the initiative and make the hard decisions, even if they end up being wrong. To a critical thinker, it is much preferable to not making a decision at all.

Critical thinkers are also honest. Moral integrity, global citizenship practices, and ethical consideration and action are all traits that you can find in a critical thinker. Honesty is found in each of these things. We see in such people a strong desire for fulfillment and harmony in the world, and part of being able to attain this will involve pursuing honesty in all relationships and endeavors that we try out.

As a critical thinker, you must always strive to use honesty in the things that you do. It isn't going to help you come up with truth and integrity and a good conclusion if you try to build it upon lies and falsehoods. When you are working on your critical thinking skills, you need to make sure that you are not only dealing with honesty when you talk to others but that you search out the truth and honesty at all times in the information that you are given.

There are a number of key considerations that can include flexibility and willingness for a critical thinker. These can be included in, but certainly are not limited, to things like the ability to:

1. Learn from your own shortcomings and mistakes.
2. Challenge the status-quo if they see that there is a need.

3. Be open-minded and learn how to embrace others' opinions and views, even if these end up challenging their own views and opinions.
4. At times, reconsider and even make some revisions to your own opinion if you are shown new evidence that may contradict what you are basing your conclusions on.
5. Listen in an active manner. Critical thinkers do not enter into a conversation just waiting for their own turn to talk, without actually listening to what others say.
6. Always learn, always improve, and always excel.

And, of course, you will find that critical thinkers are very creative in their thinking as well. Creativity is very important when it comes to the modern workforce and when it comes to our personal lives as well. Critical thinking in professional, marketing, and business alliances often relies on your ability to be creative. When businesses get a chance to be creative with their own products and even add in different ways of creativity in the way these products are advertised, they are more likely to do well.

Examples of Critical Thinking

When it comes to critical thinking, a lot of examples and ways can be used to help improve your life. You can use it at work to come up with new solutions to problems that are troubling everyone. You can use it as a way to think through all of the different scenarios that you encounter in your life so you make decisions that are the most informed. There are very few instances where critical thinking wouldn't serve you well. Some examples of when you would be able to benefit from critical thinking include:

1. If you encounter a friend who is angry, you can use critical thinking to help you interpret what that person needs. Even though that person is mad, they are still showing their needs through their comments and emotions. A critical thinker can step in and determine what the person actually needs, rather than just getting upset by it all.
2. A manager may encounter a dispute between a few employees and decide that they need to be as objective as they can. They will listen to both

sides and weigh them out using critical thinking to provide a fair option for all sides.

3. A team of scientists who are working on a complex experiment needs to have great precision. This helps them to gather and analyze data to help them out.
4. A creative writer may need to use these skills to organize all of the ideas they have for a plot of a story. They need to keep a lot of things in line when it comes to the motivations that show up and the various personalities of fictional characters.
5. A person who is running a small business has to use a lot of research and their own critical thinking to determine any possible human and economic consequences of various ways to reduce costs and increase sales.
6. A student who needs to be able to correctly explain the methodology that they used in order to come up with their conclusion.
7. An educator using various questions to ensure that their students are going to get new insights from the lesson.
8. Judges, juries, lawyers, crime scene analysts, and police detectives taking the time to

investigate, interrogate, and do the rest of the things that are needed in order to serve justice.

9. An applicant who takes the time to prepare themselves for an interview may have to use critical thinking to explain their skills and experiences and why they should be hired for the job.

10. Any parent who is trying to anticipate the costs of having a family or sending their child to college. They may do an analysis of their projected income and then budget to put money aside for this cost.

11. A financial planner can use their critical thinking skills to anticipate the impact of new income tax legislation on the tax liabilities of their client.

Thinking Hiccups

There are a lot of different things that can cause issues when it is time to think in a critical manner. Perhaps we don't understand the whole situation completely and we have decided to let that block our judgment. Maybe we come into the situation with a negative outlook from the start, and we refuse to let our biases sit to the side. Maybe there was some kind of traumatic event that came into play that changed our perceptions and made it hard for us to think in a critical fashion.

Most experts agree that there are four main roadblocks that can stop us from thinking things through in a more critical manner. Sometimes, these will create some negative feelings about getting more involved in the process of critical thinking.

The first major roadblock is that we feel critical thinking is more of a negative process. We may feel that this type of thinking is going to just tear down ideas, without inserting something in place of those original ideas. In actuality, this critical thinking is a very positive process. It helps us to take a look at the ideas that we are presented with in a more realistic way. We can then determine, without as many biases, whether we would like to believe those ideas or not.

Another issue is that we think critical thinking will make it impossible to make any commitments to ideas or people in our lives. We think that we will spend so much time thinking critically that there is no way that we could commit to others and have meaningful relationships. In reality, you can still make commitments to others; these commitments just become more informed than before so we're not only helping others, but we also agree with ones that fit our own needs and benefit us as well.

You may find that some people will see critical thinking is more of a traumatic change. The reason for this is that we think we need to always abandon old assumptions to think this way. But in reality, you can keep all of the old beliefs that you want when you start thinking in a critical manner. You will learn how to make decisions that are more informed, rather than just being consumed by your original beliefs. You don't have to give up anything; you can now just back them up with proof because you have thought things out.

And finally, another issue that many people have with critical thinking is that they think this involves being cold, unemotional, and detached. There are many critical thinkers out there who are compassionate and emotional towards others. You can easily do the same. Critical thinking can actually help you be more compassionate and helpful to others, and many find that it is liberating compared to their old way of thinking. This is often due to the fact that critical thinking allows us to free ourselves from our past assumptions and frees us from the anxiety we feel with self-scrutiny.

How Can Critical Thinking Benefit You?

Critical thinking is much more than a concept. It is a real-life model that you can use in order to build up efficient and successful problem-solving skills in your own life. You will be amazed at how much these new skills can benefit you in the workplace, in your personal life, and more. While critical thinking can be a system that is misjudged as a type of criticism, this is far from the truth. In fact, critical thinking allows you to be more open as you'll more than often want to take your time gathering all the facts before you make any decisions.

There are a lot of benefits that you can enjoy when it comes to critical thinking. The first one is that this is a crucial learning development that allows you to be more aware of the different approaches you can take to solve one problem. Without critical thinking, you are most likely to go with the method of problem-solving that is the easiest or the one that is seen as most standard. But with this skill, you will be able to find other approaches, sometimes ones of more value.

The critical thinking mindset allows you to save time. With this mindset, you will already know that all the information out there isn't going to be that important or relevant to your decision-making process. While some people are not sure how to filter out the relevant content and information from the irrelevant stuff. Critical thinking makes it easier to prioritize your time and resources by analyzing the information and finding what is most essential to the process. This can help to speed up the process while also allowing you to make a decision that is the best for your needs.

As a critical thinker, you will be able to gain an appreciation for all different types of viewpoints. This is because, even if you don't believe the same thing as others, you can learn how to empathize with the point of view that they have. Critical thinking enables you to see beyond your cultural norms, without judging them, so you can learn the different factors that may influence your own decision-making process, as well as others.

Another benefit of critical thinking is better communication. By using this skill to analyze and build up evidence for any given premise, critical thinking ensures that you become a more effective communicator than before. Having consistent and relevant points to ensure you can support the theory you are following can be very important in communicating with other people.

Of course, when you work with this, you also increase your own decision-making abilities. You will keep the guesswork and the intuition out of the mix. These may be right in some cases, but without facts to back them up, they are just guesses and are not a part of the critical thinking process. Instead, you begin to work on a more analytical and considered basis, which ensures that you have sounder decisions.

Something that you can gain from this also is that you will learn more reasoning. There are two types of reasoning: deductive and inductive. Critical thinking will teach you how to pick the right one for the situation. Grounding decisions in logic and reason, rather than on your instincts and your emotions, which can vary, will ensure that you are effective at problem-solving no matter the situation.

As you can see, there are a lot of different benefits that come with critical thinking. Every person who decides to challenge themselves to become a better and more effective thinker, and can dedicate themselves to these new skills will be able to experience all of these benefits for themselves as well.

Can I Really Use Critical Thinking?

Yes, everyone can use critical thinking in their lives. This kind of thinking ensures that you can handle any situation that comes your way, and make it easier for you to handle any situation in a fair and objective manner. You will be amazed at how well this kind of thinking can benefit your life if you just learn how to develop this skill.

There will be times when critical thinking is beneficial to you, and other times you may find that it actually slows you down. Understanding which one fits into each category can be a great sign of a critical thinker. For example, when it comes to picking out the outfit that you want to wear for the day, you don't really need to employ the skills you are learning with critical thinking. Just pick out the outfit you like the best or the one that makes the most sense for what you are doing that day.

There are many situations that can utilize your thinking skills. Being able to employ some of the skills we discuss in this guidebook and to utilize critical thinking properly can help to take a ton of weight of your shoulders. For example, if you encounter a big problem in production at work, you may need to employ critical thinking in your life. If you are trying to decide which college you want to go to, where you want to live, or what career you want to pursue when you have a few options, then critical thinking can be useful.

An effective critical thinker knows when they need to employ this kind of thinking and when it is best used to make a decision without the need to over think. This ensures that you will actually make the right decisions in your life, without having to worry about wasting a ton of time in the process.

The Main Components of Critical Thinking

Every process is usually made up of essential components, and critical thinking is exactly the same.

These components provide you a structure to the process, which, if incorporated the right way, makes persuasive, truthful, and supportive verbal communication possible to the high influence, others' points of view, and message acceptance.

There are several different components that come with critical thinking including: perception, assumptions, emotion, language, argument, fallacy, logic, and problem-solving. Let's take a look at each of these components and what they can mean when it comes time to your thinking process.

- ❖ **Perception:** The first component that comes with critical thinking is perception. This is the way in which individuals can receive, interpret, and then translate the experiences they have. How each individual perceives things around them will define how they are able to think through a situation. The past history that you have, your current mood, and the way a situation is framed can often influence your perception. Perception is interesting because it often provides individuals with a filtering system.

- ❖ **Emotion:** No matter how hard you work to think in a critical manner, your emotions will come into play at least a little bit. Your emotions are a part of everything that you do and everything that you think. Emotions are the biggest cause of creating and putting into place the operating and thinking barriers. These barriers can often be used as a way to defend us against the world. Whether that is healthy or not maybe dependent on the situation, but the emotions still have some say in how this goes. Critical thinkers don't have to ignore these emotions, and they don't even need to deny that the emotions are there. They just need to learn how to manage and accept these emotions.
- ❖ **Language:** Your thinking can't be separated out from the language. Both of these have three main purposes that go together and these include to explain, to inform, and to persuade. Language denotes (or designates meanings) and connotes (or implies or suggests something to the other person), and it relies on a lot of metaphors in order to get the job done.

- Metaphors can be very powerful tools in language, and in some cases, when they are used properly, they can even influence the way that an individual thinks and solves a problem. These tools in speech can sometimes give a lot more depth and color to your language compared to other things. Metaphors can be many different things including poetic renditions, stories, and short phrases. Understanding how others use these tools and these different types of languages can help you to take a step back from them and determine whether there is actually something of value being said or not, and whether you should follow what they say or not.
- **Argument:** For our purposes here, an argument is a claim used to persuade the other person that something is either true or untrue. It can sometimes be used to persuade someone to do something. For something to be considered an argument, there need to be three basic elements. There needs to be an issue present or one or more reasons for you to consider. There also needs to be a conclusion.

Now, just because someone presents an argument doesn't mean that it is valid. All arguments can be either be valid or invalid based on the structure that is with them, and only the premises and conclusion are reached, which can neither be false or true.

The goal you are working towards when you use critical thinking is to implement sound arguments into your life. This ensures that you have both a valid or a proper structure in your arguments and that these arguments are going to contain true premises. This is where critical thinking and all the logic make a big difference.

- ❖ **Fallacy:** If you are using reasoning that doesn't meet the criteria that has been set out for a sound argument, then that reasoning is going to be seen as erroneous or fallacious. This kind of fallacy comes when the individual uses the wrong patterns of reasoning. This doesn't always mean that they have a false conclusion, but it can underscore the fact that all of the reasoning that the individual used to support that conclusion is not valid.
- ❖ **Logic:** Logic incorporates two methods of reasoning, namely inductive and deductive.

When we take a look at deductive reasoning, we are looking at the kind that relies on validity, certainty, facts, a truth in the premises, sound arguments, and conclusions that are supported. On the other hand, inductive reasoning is a bit different because it will rely on probability, diverse facts, generalizations, and even hypotheses depending on the situation.

Often, we will use logic to help us solve the problem. Just like any other kind of problem we encounter. Using logic to solve a problem requires:

1. Understanding the problem. It means we need to listen, read, and take heed to know what is going on.
2. Identifying all of the known and the unknown, rather than trying to hide from all the unknown.
3. Interpreting any relationships that come between the known and the unknown. Sometimes, you may find that working with a visual aid can make the problem-solving easier.
4. Repeating the process any time we find it is necessary.

5. Generating a strategy to help us think logically.
6. Applying the strategy that we come up with.

Critical thinking is such an important part of our lives. If we don't take the time to increase our thinking and to become more critical about the facts that we are presented, then a lot of our beliefs may be wrong, and we may make decisions based on facts that are untrue. We will take some time later on to explore this a bit more, but understanding some of the basics of critical thinking, as we talked about in this chapter, can help us get started.

Chapter 2
Critical Thinking Test

Everyone can benefit from working on their critical thinking skills. You will find such benefits like it being easier to get along with others, able to learn the best ways to look at different solutions that are present for a problem and know how to pick the right one. You will also become more open to the different points of view you encounter from different people around you

Before you can determine where you want to go with your critical thinking skills and if there are any improvements as you work on developing your skills, you need to have a good benchmark of where you are starting. This chapter will take a look at some of the ways that you can test your own critical thinking skills and help you find ways to improve it overall.

The Critical Thinking Test

Now that we have more of an understanding about what critical thinking is all about, it is time to do some testing to see how good your own critical thinking skills are. While there are a lot of different variations on the definition that comes with critical thinking, the one that works best for our needs is this type of thinking that has the ability to comprehend the logical connections that occur between concepts, phrases, words, and ideas.

Everyone has a different level of critical thinking, and you can always work to try to improve your own thinking skills so you can develop these traits and characteristics as well. But most of us have no idea where our thinking skills are at when we first start. How are we supposed to increase our critical thinking when we have no idea where we are getting started from?

We are going to start out with some simple questions you can answer which will give you a good idea of how good your critical thinking skills can be. You can use this information to help you get a good bookmark of where you are in the beginning, then you can work from there.

Critical thinking requires the individual to learn how to recognize a pattern in the information they are given. It is especially important for that individual to recognize how the information can be connected back to the real world. Here, we are going to take a few examples to help you see how these tests work. Go ahead and try them out for yourself!

The first part will include the five words below:

1. Automobile (not a race car)
2. Walking on foot
3. Airplane
4. Bicycle
5. Cruise ship

Now, you want to start by putting them in order, from the slowest to the fastest. We will assume that they are going at their fastest speed when we do this. Go ahead and do that now, there could be different solutions to the problem. For example, you will find that the solution here has the cruise ship going faster than the car, but you may have an argument that the car is actually faster. This is known as indeterminacy and can come into play often during critical thinking.

There are also different kinds puzzles that are a little more straightforward, such as the one we have here. Take not of these words in your head:

1. Navy
2. Sky
3. Celeste
4. Azure
5. Cerulean

What do you see with these words and what do they have in common? All of the words refer to different shades of blue.

Now, take a few minutes to go through the next seven puzzles that we have here. These will hopefully be a little bit more challenging for you. We will include the answers at the end, to help you check how you are doing when it is all done.

You will want to have a pen and paper ready to note down your answers as we go along.

What do the five things listed below have in common with each other?

1. Beer
2. Orange juice
3. Soda pop
4. Coffee

5. Milk

If you took the following buildings and listed them based on their height, going from the smallest to the tallest, what would their order be?

1. Shed
2. Skyscraper
3. Duplex
4. Bungalow
5. Camping tent (a typical one, not a deluxe or special one)

What do the animals listed below have in common?

1. Mouse
2. Squirrel
3. Raccoon
4. Fox
5. Cat

Take the inventions that we have listed below and make sure to list them out in order, going from the earliest to the most recent.

1. Radio
2. Television

3. Gramophone
4. Telephone
5. Telegraph

What feature can you find with the words below that they all have in common?

1. Understand
2. Over
3. Imagination
4. Egg
5. Armchair

Looking at the bodies of water that we have below, put them in order based on their volume, starting with the smallest.

1. Lake
2. Pond
3. Ocean
4. Brook
5. Sea

When you look at the following land masses, what do you see them having in common with each other?

1. Sinai

2. Istria
3. Karpass
4. Gallipoli
5. Italy

Now that you have had some time to take a look at the questions and write down your answers, let's take a look at the answer sheet to see how much you were able to get right.

1. These are all drinkable liquids.
2. 5, 1, 4, 3, 2
3. They are all quadrupeds, and they have a tail. Also, they are all mammals.
4. 5, 4, 3, 1, 2
5. All of them start with a vowel.
6. 4, 2, 1, 5, 3
7. All of these land masses are peninsulas.

This is just a simple test that you can work with to give you a general idea of your thinking ability. But try not to worry if you struggled with this, it's not the end of the world, there are many ways you can improve your thinking skills which we will go through later in this book. If you wanted to test your ability further there are also different tests online or even with professionals that can help you look at various aspects of your critical thinking, such as your personality and how your emotions can factor into the mix as well. But this is still a great place to start to give you an idea of how your critical thinking skills are doing.

How Often Should You Test Yourself

The answer to this one varies based on how much time you spend on the techniques and how much improvement you think you are making. No matter who you are though, it is always a good idea to get started with a test right from the beginning. This can be difficult for some people because they will feel nervous about taking tests and seeing how bad their critical thinking actually is. But no one else has to see the result. This is just a number that you can use to compare yourself to other thinkers, and it may be a great way you can use to stay motived any time when things get tough.

From here, you are going to have some freedom to the number of times you want to test yourself. Testing often, in the beginning, is a good idea. Maybe consider doing a test every other week for the first few months. This can provide you with a chance to see how quickly your skills are improving and can provide you with some motivation to keep on going with the work.

Over time, as you start getting into the groove with critical thinking and you have been able to see how well your skills have improved, you can choose to limit how many times you want to further test yourself. You should do it often enough to keep yourself motivated and working, but it doesn't need to be done all the time. Many times, testing once a month or once every six weeks can be more than enough to keep you on track, and help you to see how effective your work is.

During this process, keep a notebook or something you can use to write down the critical thinking scores as you go. There will be times when you are working with this kind of process where it feels like you aren't making any progress. It is hard to remember what your score results were down the line when you want to compare things. After each test, especially for the first test that you take, make sure that you write down the answers of what you get. Even if they only provide you with a result rather than the answers, it can still help you to get the information you need to improve.

Different Types of Thinking Tests

There are many critical thinking tests that can work when it comes to testing your ability. You will want to make sure that you find an effective one that is suited for your needs. Doing research is crucial when finding the right test, so will need to be sure that you find a test that is hard enough to make your brain actually engage, and one that has a reputable research team or company behind it to make sure that this test is legitimate. Also it'll need to be long enough in order to actually provide you with some real results in the end.

You also want to take a look at whether the company provides a few different types of tests that you can choose from. Try to test yourself on a regular basis to see if your critical thinking skills are getting better. If you do the exact same test each time, you will simply start to memorize the answers, and get caught up in thinking in the same sort of thinking cycle which causes a lot of issues with the validity of the test. Or, if you end up using a different test each time, then your results are not going to be consistent between the two.

If you can find a test that has different options but comes from the same company as you used originally, this will make it easier for you to work through your techniques and the process and still test yourself on a regular basis when you want to. When you can do this, you will be more than often amazed at the results that you get, and you'll find one of the best ways to track your results and your improvements.

Are Some Tests Better Than Others?

Some of these tests are going to be easier to complete and others will be more difficult. The good thing is that you'll get the option of picking out which test you want to use. If one seems too easy for your baseline, then try something more difficult to work with.

As you are searching around for the test that you want to use, make sure that you pay attention to where they are sourced from, what kinds of questions they ask, how long they are, and even any reviews that you see. If the test looks like something for fun from a popular magazine, then you may want to avoid it and go with something else. If it comes from a popular book or from a reputable company or research group, then this is the best option for you to start with.

How Can I Tell If I'm Improving?

Taking these tests at regular intervals and writing down the results that you get will ensure that you are actually getting better with your critical thinking skills. Find a test that you rely on and stick with it. Skipping between one test to another or at least tests by different companies can mess with your end results. Since they are all different, it is likely that you are going to get varying answers to how you are doing, making it harder to tell if you are actually making progress.

In the beginning, take some time to research the different tests out there. You can even take a few of them to see which one you like the best. Once you have that, take the time to go through and work on one of the tests to get a baseline score. When you are done, write that score down so you have something to compare to later on.

Many people don't write down their score because they are worried about how low it is, or they think that they'll remember the information in their heads. Don't fret about where your critical thinking score is right now. The whole point of this guidebook is to help you improve this skill. It is less important to focus on where you are now than it is to focus on where you want to go. This result is simply so you can get an idea of where you started, and then you can see how much you increase over time.

How to Identify Critical Thinking Issues

All of us have a belief that we are great at critical thinking. We often believe that there is no chance we will be taken in by things that people tell us. We think that we are smart enough to sort through everything we see and hear and determine whether the information is true or false. We think that we can form a good argument against others, and that there is no way that we need to do more research and take more time to become a good critical thinker.

The truth is, we usually are not as good at critical thinking as we believe we are. Thinking in critical ways means that we need to assess all of our decisions and beliefs with a thorough examination. We need to seek out all the information available to us and ensure that any of the conclusions that we reach are well-reasoned. While there are biases that can and will show up sometimes, a critical thinker will understand these and avoid them, while using implication and logic to make it better and to still choose the right decision in each scenario.

You may be a good critical thinker in some areas of your life, but it is likely that one or more area is going to suffer to some extent. Here, we are going to take a look at some of the areas that critical thinkers can often have trouble with.

The first high issue area for critical thinking is self-assessment. As many studies show, humans aren't the best at judging their own progress. We often rate ourselves lower or higher than we need to most of the time, whether we are considering our skills, the knowledge that we have, or how well we did on a test. Going on your own feelings and what your emotions tell you to do can really make it hard to think in a critical way. No one has ever made the best decisions when they are highly emotional. If you ever find yourself feeling down on yourself, you may self-assess yourself less than you should, compared to if you were in a good mood, you may self-assess yourself at a higher level than you really should.

The truth is, even when you are working with critical thinking, you may find that it is hard to self-assess yourself. This is why people take before and after pictures when they are trying to lose weight, and it is the reason we take tests to look at our skills. Sometimes, we think we have come further than we have, and sometimes we think we haven't made any progress at all. Having these benchmarks and testing yourself is one of the best ways to determine if you are actually seeing progress or not.

Another thing to watch out for is the statistics and probability. Most people are not very good at judging the odds of a decision or understanding how statistics can be applied in the real world. Sure, you may have learned a few statistics and probability in math class, but when you are trying to assess the probability, you may find that the amount you want to see can be a much bigger factor than anything else. Most of the time we are not taught about using an appropriate sample size, how to deal with the outliers, and many other things needed to apply statistics in real life.

Some people run into issues with recognizing any biases they may have. If you take a look at some of the studies out there, you may notice that there is a common idea that people have trouble knowing when they are making errors in their judgment and when they are being biased. While we can quickly recognize these issues in others, sometimes, we run into trouble spotting these in ourselves which can make it to make good decisions ourselves.

When there is a bias in your thinking, it is hard to change your mind no matter how many facts you encounter that goes against it. Critical thinkers have to be willing to give up the notions they have in the beginning if there is enough evidence to prove you wrong. It is fine to have some guesses or notions in the beginning, but holding onto them just because you don't want to believe something else is not a good sign. There is nothing wrong with having a bias, and most people, no matter how hard they try, will start out with some thoughts on a subject. But the difference is that a critical thinker is still willing to take in both sides and will be willing to change their ideas if needed.

You also need to worry about how your emotions can come into play with the thoughts that you have. If your emotions are negative at the time or you are more attached emotionally to one option over another, it is harder to pick another option even if that other one is the correct one. This can be seen a lot with the relationships that we have. We may know that a relationship is toxic and bad for us, but because we are attached emotionally to that other person, we choose to stay. We may know that the other person is right with a decision, but because we don't like them or they did something to us in the past, we refuse to see reason and stick with the outside, even when it is the wrong side.

If you want to be a critical thinker, then you need to recognize how your emotions come into play and learn how to make smart decisions, despite what your emotions are saying. This doesn't mean that you can't ever feel an emotion, but as a critical thinker, you have to make sure that your emotions are not controlling the decisions that you make.

Even some of the best critical thinkers are not going to be immune to some of the issues above. Everyone can face them at some point or another. It is up to you to determine whether they keep you from making smart decisions or not. Understanding what these issues are and learning how to avoid them and work against them will ensure you make the best decisions possible.

Chapter 3
THE STEPS AND STAGES OF CRITICAL THINKING

There are many different parts that come to the process of critical thinking. You may fall into several different stages based on the way you approach a problem and its solution right now. There are also different steps that you can choose to follow when it comes to becoming a critical thinker in your own life. Let's take a look at each of these and how they all work together to come up with the best way for you to become a critical thinker.

What Are the Different Stages of Critical Thinking?

As you work on becoming a critical thinker, you will find that there are a few different stages of critical thinking that you need to consider. Depending on how far you are in the process, you may fit into one of the stages. In the beginning, you may be an unreflective thinker, but as you work on your skills, you can move into an accomplished thinker or at least an advanced thinker. With that said, there are six main stages of critical thinking, which will be explained below. These include:

1. The unreflective thinker
2. The challenged thinker
3. The beginning thinker
4. The practicing thinker
5. The advanced thinker
6. The accomplished thinker

The Unreflective Thinker

To start with is the unreflective thinker. These individuals are usually unaware of the determining role that their thinking can have in their lives. They will often run into a lot of problems because the current method of thinking they use leads them there. Unreflective thinkers may lack the ability to assess their thinking, so it is hard for them to improve it.

You will find that an unreflective thinker lacks the knowledge that they need to think critically. They may just make decisions based on their emotions or on a limited number of facts. They won't take the time to look through different points of view, assess their thinking, do research, or anything else to ensure they make the best decisions possible. In some cases, these types of thinkers can develop skills for thinking, without even being aware of it. But since these skills are applied in an inconsistent manner, it doesn't really help them out all that much.

The Challenged Thinker

A thinker can move over to being challenged when they are first seeing that their thinking is playing a role in their lives and when they are aware of the fact that the big problems that come up in their thinking can cause them significant problems. They are just starting to see the difference and starting to see that high-quality thinking means that they need to be deliberate with their way of thinking. They may see that their current way of thinking is flawed, but they may not be able to identify these flaws.

Most thinkers who fit in this stage are going to be limited when it comes to skills for thinking. They may have a few skills although they aren't aware of them and these skills will sometimes get in the way of their development of becoming more advanced thinkers. Many of these thinkers have found ways to make themselves believe their thinking is much better than it really is, which can sometimes make it more of a challenge when it comes down to trying to improve their thinking skill.

The Beginning Thinker

When an individual starts to move to this stage, they are ready to take on the challenge of improving their thinking through different domains of their lives. Thinkers who enter this stage know that they have problems with the current way that they think, and they are starting to take the right steps to better understand the ways in which they can improve their thinking. They may even might try to make modifications to their thinking, but their insight is limited right now. They may not have a good plan for improving their thinking, so many of their efforts are lacking and not that helpful.

Beginning thinkers are aware of their thinking and can even understand how their thinking plays a role in their assumptions and points, of view. They are just starting to recognize that there are many standards to asses their thinking and that all of these need to be in place to see results. These thinkers may even be able to appreciate someone critiquing their powers, and their skill level is high enough that they can start to monitor their thoughts, even though their monitoring may not be the best.

The Practicing Thinker

Thinkers who have moved into this stage usually have a sense of the habits that they would work on to be in control of their own thinking. They recognize that there are problems blocking their thinking and are ready to attack these problems in a systematic way. Based on their sense of the need to practice on a regular basis, they are actively looking at their mode of thinking on several domains. Since they are only doing this in a systematic way, though, they may be limited on their insights.

The practicing thinker has enough skill when it comes to thinking that they can now critique their own plan for systematic practice, and they can then critique their own powers of thought. They can also work to monitor their own thoughts on a regular basis. This helps them to articulate effectively their own weaknesses and strengths. They may even be able to recognize their own egocentric thinking and see the same in others.

The Advanced Thinker

Thinkers who have been able to move onto this stage are now establishing good habits or thoughts that pay off for them. Based on these new habits they have, they can analyze their thinking on all of the domains of their lives, but they are still lacking on the significant insights into problems at a deeper level of thought. They can think well across many different dimensions of their lives, but they may not be able to consistently do this.

Advanced thinkers are actively and successfully engaging in a systematic monitor of the role of their thinking in all options. They may critique their own way of doing things to ensure they think fairly and critically. They have a great knowledge of the qualities of their thinking, and they can often identify when their thinking is more egocentric than not. They may even have a few different strategies that they can use to limit how much this happens.

The Accomplished Thinker

An accomplished thinker has not only taken charge over their thinking, but they know that they need to continuously monitor their thinking, revising it, and thinking of new strategies to make it better. They have internalized the basic skills of thought so that all the critical thinking they do is now highly intuitive and easy to work with. They will do a self-assessment on a regular basis, and they know how to be fair-minded and can usually control their own egocentric nature rather than letting it take control over them.

Thinkers who fit into this category often critique their own use of thinking throughout their lives and will normally try to find a way to improve it. They can monitor the thoughts they have and know their strengths and the weaknesses of their own thinking. They still have a bit of egocentrism that sneaks into their thoughts on occasion, but they are usually able to control this, rather than letting it take over and control the way that they think altogether.

What Are the Different Steps of Critical Thinking?

We also need to look at the different stages and steps that come with critical thinking. Each day, we are faced with a multitude of problems and situations that we need to solve after a thorough evaluation, and with these situations, we are often challenged to understand the different perspectives that we need to think about to get the right solution.

Most of the time we will build up our cognitive thinking based on what has happened to us in the past. However, this doesn't always mean that we will always come up with a better solution to a problem. This may be due to the fact that a decision can be affected by the wrong facts, our emotions, or some other external influences that determine the solution we pick. This is why critical thinking tends to build on a rational, open-minded process that will depend on information and empirical evidence.

The beauty of critical thinking is that it can help us to think through the decisions rather than jumping right to a conclusion. Instead, critical thinking can guide the mind through a variety of logical steps that will ensure that we take in a larger range of perspectives, even if these are different from our own. From here, we can accept the finding, put aside the biases that we personally have, and then consider from all of the possibilities that are possible.

Now, there are six steps that you can use in order to achieve the results we have just mentioned. These include knowledge, comprehension, application, analyze, synthesis, and then to take action. Let's take a look at a brief description of each of these and some of the ways that you can implement each of these to help you become a more critical thinker.

Knowledge

For every problem that you encounter, a clear vision is one of the best ways to get on the path to solving that problem. In this step, we are going to figure out what argument or what problem needs to be solved. If we don't have a clear picture of the problem that we need to solve, how are we ever going to stand a chance of looking for the right information and figuring out the right way to solve it.

To start, you need to ask the right questions that will help you acquire a deeper understanding of the problem. You may even find that when you are asking questions, there isn't really an actual problem, which means there isn't much of a need to move forward with the other steps in your critical thinking model. Do you really want to spend a lot of time working on a problem and finding a good solution for it if there really isn't a problem there to start with?

When you are thinking about the questions that you want to ask in this question, remember that open-ended ones are the best. These allow you to really explore the problem. Answering yes or no to a question may be easier for you, but it doesn't really provide you with any of the information that you need to solve that problem. When you ask the right questions, you will give yourself a chance to discuss and explore the main reasons behind it. During this stage, there are two big questions that you must address no matter what else you ask later on: What is the problem? Why do we need to solve it?

Comprehension

Once you have taken the time to ask yourself questions and figure out what the problem is, the next thing to work on is understanding the situation and the facts that are aligned with it. You have to fully comprehend the problem and gather as many facts as you can to help you determine the best course of action. It is impossible for you to figure out a good solution if you don't even comprehend anything about the problem.

The data that you collect about the problem can be found with a lot of research. You can choose the kind of research methods that you want to use. You may also find that the deadline you get can make a difference as well. If you have a month to figure out a solution, then you may be able to explore your options more than if you are only given a few days to do the same.

Make sure that when you are doing your research, you find research that comes from many different perspectives. It isn't going to do you much good if the information that you collect only leans towards your own opinion on the matter. If you are going to do it this way, why not just pick your solution from the start and save time? A critical thinker wants to be able to find the best solution, regardless of what that solution is. So, try to find a lot of different perspectives to help you make all decisions.

Application

This step is going to continue on with the previous step to help you get a complete understanding of the different facts that are aligned with it and the data that you took the time to collect concerning the problem, using whichever research method that you want. You can then take this research and use it to solve the problem at hand by building up links between the resources and the information.

You may find that a mind map can also be helpful when you want to analyze the situation. A mind map is type of visual diagram using a bunch of ideas that all lead to one central overall idea. You can then use the information on your mind map to come up with the best solution.

Analyze

Once you have taken the time to gather the information and have linked together everything that you can between the main problems, it is time to analyze the situation. You will want to take some time to look at the strong points, all of the weak points, and the challenges faced when it comes to solving the problem. You can also use this time to set up the right priorities for your main cause so that you can determine the best way to address them in the solution.

This part can take some time. During this time, you will need to find tools that you can use to make the analyses easier to work on. For example, one tool that can be used to help with this step is the cause-effect diagram. This divides the problem away from the causes of the problem aiming to identify all of the different causes so that they can be categorized based on their type and how much they actually impact the problem at hand.

If you are dealing with a big problem, you may need to take more time to analyze. The cause and effect chart may be bigger than you anticipated.

Synthesis

When we reach this stage, we will have taken the proper time to fully analyze all of the problem and have considered all of the information related to it. We can now work on forming a decision on how to solve the problem. As we come up with a solution, we can look at the initial routes to follow to make this decision so we can put it into action.

You may find that with some of the more complex problems, there could be several solutions. If you see that there are a few solutions to a problem, you need to evaluate them and then prioritize which one seems like the best option to help you pick the right one. Depending on how big a problem this is, you can use a

SWOT analysis or something similar to it in order to identify the strength, weakness, opportunity, and threats to each solution.

Take Action

The final step that we need to look at here is taking action. By now, you should have come up with a solution that you can put into action in order to handle the problem. You can then take the result of your critical thinking and turn it into actionable steps. If you find that the decision involves a certain project or team, then you need to go through and do a plan of action to make sure that the right solution is adopted and executed the way that you would like.

Now, sometimes, you will have a fair bit of time to go through all of these steps. You can take a few days or even a few weeks to consider all of the different options that are available and go from there. Other times, you may just have a matter of minutes to make a decision based on the information that you have been given and your situation. Regardless of the amount of time that you have to make a decision, you can still work with the basics of critical thinking to come up with a good solution. The only thing that'll differ is the time you'll get to do research and analysis. But as you learn to adapt to this thinking process, you will eventually be able to make faster decisions as well.

Chapter 4

How to Develop Your Thinking Skills

At this point, you should now have a good idea of what critical thinking is all about. You know that it is important to help you get the results that you want in making the best decisions to improve your life, and that there are also different steps and stages that come with critical thinking.

We are now going to take a look at some of the best practical ways that you can develop your critical thinking skills in your everyday life to get the best results possible.

Ask Basic Questions

The first thing that you can work on is asking basic questions about any problem or situation that occurs in your life. Sometimes, the explanation of something becomes so convoluted and complex that you lose out on the original question that you should be asking. In order to make sure that you are avoiding this, you continually need to go back to the basic questions that you asked when you first made it your goal to find a solution to the problem.

Every problem that you encounter along the way has a different set of questions that you can ask. You should always ask more and more questions to help you out. The more questions that you can ask about a specific problem, the more viewpoints you can get for it, and the easier it becomes to see the right solution show up. But some of the key questions that you can ask to get yourself started no matter what the problem include:

1. What am I overlooking about this problem?
2. What information do I already know?
3. How do I know this information? Am I able to trust this source?
4. What am I looking to prove or disprove or critique with this problem?

Question Some of Your Basic Assumptions

Some of the best innovators throughout history were those individuals who were able to look up for a moment and wonder if the assumptions that everyone else were using were actually wrong. When you question the assumptions that you and others make, this is when innovation is going to happen. Of course, you don't have to be an Einstein or anything to benefit from making a question the assumptions that are out there. What about that trip that you have wanted to take? The hobby that you want to try? The internship that you wanted to get?

All of these things can actually become a reality for you, but you do need to step out of your comfort zone, question your assumptions and then critically evaluate your beliefs about what is possible, appropriate, and prudent.

You always want to be careful about the assumptions you are making in your regular life. There are a lot of assumptions out there about a lot of things and just following along with them, without taking the time to review why those assumptions are there and whether they are right or wrong, can lead to a lot of problems. Sometimes, the assumptions are right. But more often than not, they are wrong. Realizing this and looking for a better solution can be one of the best things you can do.

Being Aware of Your Mental Processes

Human thought is pretty amazing. But the automation and the speed that happens in some cases with this thought process can be a disadvantage to us when we want to think in a critical manner. Sure, it was there to help us survive and do well in the past. But now that we are in a time and age where we aren't always in danger, this kind of mental process doesn't always serve us the best overall.

Our brains are set up to use mental shortcuts, also known as heuristics, to help explain what is going on around us. This happens automatically, even if we don't actively think about it. This was very beneficial to us when we were fighting off animals and hunting large game. But when we need to take the time to think through something critically, it can be a disaster.

As a critical thinker, you need to be aware of this cognitive bias and the personal prejudice that we have. We need to realize that this can make it hard to be objective and come up with the actual best solutions and decisions. All of us are born with this bias when it comes to our thinking, and it's not something that we can fully avoid. But when we become aware of these issues and work to fight against them, it can help drastically towards improving your thinking ability.

Try Reversing Things

If you are stuck on a hard problem and you just can't seem to find the right solution to solving it, then one thing that you will want to try out is reversing things. For example, you may find that it is obvious that X causes Y, but why not look and see what would happen if Y caused X.

A good example of this issue is the chicken and the egg problem. At first, it may seem like the chicken coming first is the obvious answer. The chicken is responsible for laying the egg so it makes sense to think this way. but then you stop and think that the chicken had to come from somewhere, and since chickens come straight from eggs, it also makes sense that the egg had to be the first to come.

In some cases, this will answer the problem and you will even be able to come up with the best solution a lot easier. Of course, there will be times when the reverse is not true. But taking the time to consider it can help you change your way of thinking, and it may be just the trick that you need to actually find the right solution.

Evaluate the Evidence That You Have

Any time that you are working to solve a problem, you will find that it can be helpful to look at other information that others have done previously in the same area. It is likely that someone, at some point, has encountered the same problem, and this will be able you to see a lot of the information and research that you need to make a good solution. There really isn't a reason for you to go through and start solving a new problem from scratch, especially when others have already been able to do a lot of the work on that problem for you ahead of time.

You are likely to find a ton of information and research out there that you can use when it comes to evaluating the problem. However, it is also important for you to take a critical look at the information that you find. Not all of the information is going to be informative, not all of it will be complete, and not all of it will actually be truthful. There is often a lot of bias out there when it comes to the information that you want to use, and you must be aware of this.

For example, you may find that there is an article out there that bashes the benefits of one natural remedy or natural medication that you can use for diabetes or blood pressure. It may sound convincing, and if you just looked at the document, you may believe that you need to stay as far away from that natural solution as possible. But then you take a closer look and find that the researchers who did the study were funded by a big diabetes medication company, and now you know that maybe the medication isn't so bad, but maybe it will cut into the profits of the big company.

When you find evidence that you want to use or evaluate, you need to ask questions. Look at who took the time to gather the evidence. Look at the way that they gathered the evidence, and then ask why they gathered this information. This can go a long way in helping you determine whether the information is a good source to work from, or whether you need to find something with less bias in it. Finding out the information to these questions doesn't automatically discredit them, but it lets you know whether there is any form of bias in the information before you choose to use it.

Always Think for Yourself

While we have spent some time talking about the importance of research when it comes to critical thinking, make sure that you don't become so bogged down in reading and research that you decide to just use someone else's thinking, rather than your own. You always need to think for yourself. In fact, this can quickly become one of your most powerful tools.

Sometimes, the best way to make a decision is to not listen to the opinions of someone else. This can get you bogged down and, in some cases, you may find that the emotional ties of a certain situation can make it really hard to find someone who isn't biased. Thinking on your own and using the information that you already have at your disposal, instead of looking for other opinions, can be the best bet.

In fact, even Einstein thought that this could be the best way to think about situations over others. C. P. Snow, after writing about Einstein for some time, observed that it was like Einstein "had reached the conclusions by pure thought, unaided, without listening to the opinions of others". This was in regard to Einstein's paper "On the Electrodynamics of

Moving Bodies". If Einstein chose to come up with his own conclusions without taking a look at the opinions of others, then so can you.

Of course, this doesn't mean that you should be overconfident. There are times when you still need to bring out the research of others and listen to other opinions to help you with your own decisions. But you can also recognize that thinking for yourself is really important when it comes to answering some of the tough questions that you must deal with. Knowing the right times to deal with each one can make a big difference in how well you are able to think critically.

Not Always Needing to Think Critically

Thinking critically is so important when it comes to making the right decisions for your own life. It can help you to make decisions that will benefit you and can even help in building your professional and personal relationships. However, you won't be able to think critically in every situation you encounter.

It is fine to not think about each and every decision critically. But critical thinking is an important tool that you can use. Just like other skills and tools that you may work on in your life, it is one that you should deploy when you need to solve really difficult problems or when you must make important decisions. But this doesn't mean that you need to take the time and energy to think critically about every decision.

For example, there is no reason to think critically about what you will have for lunch. Unless you have some sort of food allergies, you can just make a decision based on how hungry you are, what is nearby, and what sounds good. Most people decide their lunch in just a few minutes or less, and this is perfectly fine. It's unlikely that the one meal out of thousands in your life will make that big of a difference.

But when it comes to making big decisions, such as changing to a new job, deciding where to live, buying a home, and so on, then critical thinking can be very important. It is your job as a critical thinker to figure out the best times to think critically and the times when it may not be as necessary.

Chapter 5

QUESTIONS TO APPLY IN CRITICAL THINKING

When it comes to critical thinking, asking lots of questions can help you get the results you need. The more questions that you ask, the easier it will be for you to figure out all of the possible solutions to an issue. When you are picking out questions, you must make sure that you apply questions that are open-ended. It isn't going to do you much good if all of your questions can be answered as yes and no. Doing this will only limit the answers that you get back and the information that you find out.

It is always best to use questions that require you to think, take a little time to discuss, and need more than one-word answers to complete. You can always utilize the five why's that we talked about earlier, or you can find another method that works the better for you, as long as you ask lots of questions and ensure that they need a lot of discussions to go with them.

The type and number of questions that you choose to ask will directly relate to the problem you are dealing with. Some may work well using the five why's helping you to get the answers you need to solve the problem. Other times, you may need to make more time in order to answer more questions to find the solution. Critical thinkers know that the first solution they come up with or the first question that you ask won't give you the best solution possible most of the time. Asking more questions to help you with the certainty of the answers that you get can help you out a lot. Let's take a look at some of the questions that you can ask when it comes to critical thinking.

Knowledge

The first part that we are going to look at is the knowledge questions. This is going to allow the individual to exhibit information that they have learnt in the past. They simply can do this by recalling basic concepts, terms, recalling facts, and answers. Some of the questions that you can ask that fit into this category include:

1. How would you describe…?
2. Why did…?

3. How would you explain..?
4. When did X happen?
5. What is…?

Comprehension

It is also possible for you to use your comprehension with these questions. Being able to demonstrate an understanding of facts and ideas can be possible with the help of organization, translation, comparison, interpretation, and giving descriptions. You can also use this as a way to state your ideas. When your able to use all of the other options, you will get better at stating your ideas because you have the facts to back yourself up. Some of the questions that you can use that fit into this category include:

1. What evidence is there?
2. What ideas or facts do we have?
3. Explain the situation or the answers in your own words.
4. How would you compare or contrast?

Application

Now, it is time to move onto the application of the solution and some of the questions that you need to ask to make this work. Being able to solve problems by applying any of the knowledge that you acquired can be a part of this. You also have to take a different view of the rules, techniques, and facts that you encounter during this time as well. Some of the questions that you can ask when you are in the application part of the process include:

1. What might happen if I do X?
2. What approach would be the best to do X?
3. How would you show how well you understand X?
4. What examples can you find?

Analysis

During the analysis, you will take a look at all of the information and research that you looked for to examine and break down information into smaller parts. This helps you to identify motives and causes. You can also spend this time making inferences and find evidence that will support your generalizations.

Some of the questions that you can ask when you are looking through this analysis category include:

1. Are you able to identify the different parts of the category?
2. What is the best way to categorize X?
3. Are you able to classify X?
4. Are you able to make any inferences?

Evaluation

During this category, you will need to present and then defend your opinions by making judgments about the information you have, the validity of ideas that you are looking at, and the quality of work based on the criteria that you set. Some of the questions that you can ask when it comes to the evaluation category include:

1. What would you recommend to someone else if you had been…?
2. What was the value or the importance of…?
3. What is the contribution of X to the whole process?
4. Which option do you feel is the best?
5. How would you compare X to other options?

Creation and Synthesis

At some point, you will need to be creative with the solution that you have. This part requires that you compile together information in a different way than before. You can do this by taking the elements that you have and combining them into a new pattern. You can even spend some time proposing new and alternative solutions that others may not have considered in the past. Some of the questions that you can consider for this section include:

1. Is there a marmite solution that you can go with here?
2. Are you able to propose an alternative interpretation to that of X? what might have happened if?

Asking a ton of questions during this process is going to help you to come up with new solutions that can work well for your problem. You never want to stop with just one or two questions. This may provide you with one or two solutions, but this doesn't guarantee that you are going to find the best one. Asking questions about different things and looking at the problem in different ways can ensure that you will be able to find the solutions that you want and need for that particular problem.

Chapter 6
DECISION-MAKING

Another aspect that we need to talk about when it comes to critical thinking is your decision-making abilities. Critical thinking isn't going to do you much good if you cannot put it to work in making the best decisions for you. This chapter will help shed some light on decision-making and why it is so important aspect that you need to master in your daily life.

What Is Decision-Making?

For the most part, decision-making helps you to solve any problem that you encounter, whether it happens in your personal life or in your professional life. You will do this by examining all the choices at your disposal and then deciding on the best way to fix that problem. Many people find that using a step-by-step approach is a great way to make thoughtful and informed decisions that will have a positive impact on you.

There are seven basic steps that can be utilized in the decision-making process, no matter what kind of decision you are trying to make. These seven steps include the following:

1. **Identify the decision:** You first need to stop and recognize the problem and make a decision that actually addresses the nature of the problem. Determine why this decision is going to be so important so you can stay on the right track from the beginning.
2. **Gather the necessary information:** The next thing to work on is to gather any and all information needed so that you can make smart decisions based on relevant data and facts. This will usually take some work. You need to look at the information and determine if it has any value, if it is relevant to the decision you want to make, and whether you need more information or not. During this stage, ask yourself what is needed to make the right decisions, and then seek out anyone else who may need to be involved in the decision-making process.
3. **Identify all of the alternatives:** Once you have taken the time to get a clear understanding of the issue, it is time to look at all the different

solutions that are present. No matter what the decision, it's likely that there will be several solutions. You can take a look at the options at this point and use that to determine the best course of action at this time.

4. **Weigh all the evidence:** After you have the different solutions at your disposal, it is time to weigh the evidence and determine which solutions will actually be the best for you. For each solution, you will want to go through and weigh the pros and the cons, and then pick out the option that will provide you with the least amount of risk. You may also want to consider a second opinion during this time.

5. **Choose your solution:** When you reach the time to make a decision, make sure that you really know the risks with each chosen route. It may even be possible to choose a combination of alternatives if the information and the risks point to this being the best option.

6. **Take action:** The point of doing these steps is for you to be able to take the necessary action needed. Once you pick out a good solution, you will need to come up with a good plan for implementation. This can include identifying

what resources are required and then getting the right support that is needed, if this is necessary.

7. **Review the decision:** After the solution has had time to be implemented, it is time to evaluate how effective the decision is. You can then make any improvements that are needed.

At times, decision-making can be hard, and you will find yourself struggling to stick with one over another. You will want to make sure that you are picking out the solution that works best for you. We always want to find a way to use the solution that has the lowest amount of risk and the biggest amount of positives for us. Then, there are times when the emotions come into play or the one with the least amount of risk is harder to accomplish, and we may often struggle against that in the hopes of finding a better solution.

Following the steps that we just talked about to come up with the best solution will ensure that you actually find and stick with a good decision when your deciding on something. Having this systematic method of looking for the best solution will also help you to keep emotions out of the way.

Although the steps that we have just mentioned make it easier to come up with the most effective decisions, there are still a few pitfalls that you may need to watch out for. The first one is that you either have too little or too much information. Gathering the right information is so important when you start with the decision-making process. As a critical thinker, it is your job to figure out how much of this background information you truly need. Too little and it is hard to make a smart decision; too much and you may feel overwhelmed often leading you to confusion which will prevent you from making the decision that you need.

Another issue that you may encounter is that you misidentify the problem. Most of the time, you will be able to correctly see the issues around the decision. However, there may be times when the decision is more complex, and you will have trouble figuring out where this main issue is. Take the time to speak with experts, conduct research, and more to help you figure out the right problem. This, in the long run, is going to save you a ton of resources and time.

Sometimes, the issue that you will face with your decision-making is that you are overly confident in the outcome you will get. Even if you go through all of the steps we have talked about, there is a chance that the outcome won't turn out the way you want. Being overconfident can lead you to making mistakes and make it harder for you to handle if the solution doesn't end up being the one that you've expected.

Things That Can Affect Your Decision-Making

There are a lot of different things that can come into play with your decision-making abilities. You have to be very careful when you are trying to make important decisions because there are a lot of things that can come into play that will help you to make better decisions, or that can also make it hard for you to work on your decision-making abilities.

The first thing that can affect your decision-making abilities is your emotions. When you let your emotions out to play, you are less likely to make the decisions that are right for you. Instead, you will choose things based on whether you like someone or not, or make decisions in the heat of the moment, often with no thought or logic behind it. Learning how to make decisions without the emotions is so important when you are a critical thinker.

Another issue to watch out for is whether you have the right kind of information, and the right amount, to help with making a decision. If you try to make a decision without any information at all, or if you pick out information that is wrong or biased, you will often have a lot of trouble making the right decision. You should always be careful when it comes to your decision-making process to ensure you actually have the facts that you need.

Your physical comfort can also affect the decision-making process. If you are tired, hungry, uncomfortable, or in pain, then you may need to work on fixing these issues. Your mind is going to head right over to the physical ailments before it tries to make any important decisions. So, take a nap if you are tired. If you are hungry, eat something beforehand and make sure you get a drink. Work to reduce the amount of discomfort you have before you work on any major decision.

If you are tired or fatigued from making a lot of decisions, it can affect your decision-making skills as well. If you have spent all day thinking things through and coming up with decisions about various problems, your mind will tend to glaze over. It may be wise to put off the decision-making for a while and take time out so you can give your mind a break to ensure your mind can go back to being fully optimal when it comes to thinking and making decisions.

How to Make a Decision

We run into making choices each day. There are times when we choose the wrong things, and there are times when we struggle to make a decision at all in the first place. If you find that this is a problem you are dealing with, then it is time for you to learn some techniques that will help you in making better decisions. Some of the steps that you can take in order to increase your decision-making skills include:

Determine What You Have at Stake

There are a lot of decisions you need to make in your life. Choices can range from something huge that can change your life all the way to something as simple as trying to pick what to wear in the morning. Being able to determine the weight of all your decisions can make it easier to complete these decisions. This is a pretty basic aspect of thinking you can apply. If the decision is a big choice, then it requires some research and more careful consideration. Smaller decisions, such as what to wear in the morning, can just be done on blind faith and what you prefer because there isn't as much weight placed on those. Ask yourself a question in these situations such as: "Is this really a big decision that I need more time to think about? or am I over thinking this as it's something that doesn't really matter too much?"

Why Are You Making the Decision?

There are certain agendas and reasonings that can effect the overall decision that you come to make. To help determine who the decision is for and who may benefit from the decision the most, you have to really think through it and consider the decision from many different angles.

This again brings up the idea of asking a lot of questions. First, ask if there are any other reasons why you need to make this decision. Is there anyone in particular who will benefit if you make a certain decision over another one? All of this information can make it easier for you to help you achieve the reason for making a decision and may even make it easier when it comes to choosing the right one also.

Determine the Number of Choices You Have

With a lot of the decisions that you need to make, there is going to be at least two choices that you can choose from. And more than often, these choices can even be hidden. For example, even if you are doing something as simple as picking out a flavor of ice cream, you get to choose between two or more flavors that you like. You can try to organize your different options into what will work, what you don't think will work, and what might be able to work. Once this is laid out, this will help you to look at everything objectively before making decisions.

Make Your Decisions Informed

Before you make any kind of decision you can ask questions of someone who has to make the decision with you, or you can just spend time asking questions in general. Your job is to take in as much information as possible before you decide on anything.

For example, a good thing to consider is who is going to benefit the most if you make one decision over another? If you were leaning towards one decision over another, why is that? Will one decision end up with more work to complete compared to others? The point of asking these questions is to think things through before you make any sort of choice at all.

Consider a Second Opinion

Making certain decisions can be hard. The good news is that you don't have to always make the decisions on your own. You can always benefit from getting a second opinion. If you look for a second opinion, make sure that this opinion is from someone you trust. This person can be your friend, a family member, or even an expert you can call if you have these connections.

The point here is to get the opinion from someone who may be separate to the actual problem. They may be able to look at it from a different point of view and can discuss the various options with you. Even if you don't pick the decision that you get from them, asking someone else to help you with decisions can help you pick the best choice overall.

Decide with Logic and Leave the Emotion Behind

There will be some instances where we will get caught up in the moment letting our emotions get the better of us. When this happens, we usually start to make rash and ill-advised decisions due to pride, sadness, and even anger. When it comes to making good decisions, your emotions can have a very dangerous influence on you. This is because you are going to just jump on the first decision that pops into your head, without thinking it through.

Before you decide to make any decisions, it is important to take a break and ensure that your emotions are not causing any issues and messing with your logic. Before you decide, take a deep breath and work on clearing your mind so that the emotions never get in the way of your judgment. Once you are sure those emotions are gone or have subsided, your logic should be clear and you're ready to move forward from this point.

Learn from Your Bad Decisions

No matter how hard you work on your critical thinking, there will always be times when you make decisions that are often not the right ones. This is just a part of life. But that shouldn't stop us from thinking carefully on the next problem we face. There are so many decisions that we have to make in our daily lives, and it is impossible for us to pick the right choice each time. What we need to do here is to be ready to accept failure when it happens. Yes, accepting failure can be hard to handle. No one likes it. But when you learn how to accept it and take it gracefully, you can learn a lot that will help you to make the right choices in the future.

How to Make Better Decisions

All of us want to the ability and confidence to make better decisions in our lives. Learning how to improve our decision-making skills so that we can make the best choices is something that we'd all love to do. Here are some of the ways that you can ensure to make better decisions in your day to day life:

1. **Make all the decisions in the morning.** Morning is often the best time to make some of your biggest decisions. This is due to the benefit of having a combination of dopamine and serotonin which helps avoid the issue of decision fatigue. If you do need to make a

bigger decision later on in the day, then taking a nap or at least taking a break can help to reset the brain.
2. **Eat first.** Making decisions when you are hungry can be almost impossible. It affects the way you think. Try to get all of your physical desires taken care of before you start on your daily work or tasks.
3. **Cut down how many choices you get.** Sometimes, we get overwhelmed when we have too many choices to decide on. Limiting ourselves to just a few choices as soon as possible can ensure that making a decision is much easier.
4. **Open up the windows.** Adding some extra oxygen to the home can help you to make better decisions, and also adding plants around the house can help aswell.

Decision-Making in the Workplace and Life

While there are a lot of important decisions that you will need to make in your own personal life, there are also a lot of times when you must make critical decisions in your workplace. This can be difficult a lot of the time due to the people your work with. Whether it is a big business or a small one, there are always others who will need to agree to the decisions so everyone can work together on the decision being implemented.

It is important that the information is shared between everyone, and that everyone gets a chance to vote and give their opinion before any decision is agreed upon. Some of the steps that you can take in order to ensure strong and sound decisions are made in the workplace include:

1. **Decide how important the decision is.** Our modern world is always busy and many things feel rushed. We get into the mindset that each decision has to be done right now, as soon as possible. But in reality, some decisions need more time than others. Take a step back from the problem and then decide how urgent and important the decision really is.
2. **Consider a large range of options for decision-making.** Depending on the project, you may want to work with a consensus, a vote, or a subgroup or a single person to decide. All

of them can be effective, but you will have to decide what is the best option for you and the situation you're in.

3. **Make sure that you define things up front.** This should be done especially if you are working with a consensus. For example, you may decide that you are going to continue on with a debate and the exploration until everyone is fully supportive of the final decision. In some cases, they can drag on for some time. Or, if you find that you have a limited time for the decision-making, you may want to put a deadline on reaching a consensus.

4. **Make sure the right people are in the process.** You should include those who are going to make the decision, along with those who are going to implement the solution and anyone else who will be affected by the solution and the decision.

5. **Make all of the data that you have available.** You may find that you don't have all the data, but make sure that all of the data that you have is out in the open to help you make an informed a decision. If you feel that you are stuck, then you need to look for more research.

If possible, also look at the data that includes the sense of security, wishes, and fears of those in the business. All of these can play into the decision that you go with.

6. **Estimate a deadline for the decision.** You should also consider letting others know the deadline ahead of time. If you find that the decision needs to be delayed, then make sure that you update others. And once you find that the decision is made, ensure that everyone knows what it is.

7. **Expect that there will be some struggle.** No matter what the situation is and the decision you make, expect that there will be some sort of struggle involved. It isn't easy to get through this, but it is a valuable part of the process and one that you shouldn't just skip over.

Techniques to Improve Your Decision-making Abilities

Decision-making is an important part of our lives. We are constantly surrounded by decisions that we need to follow all of the time. Whether we are deciding on a big move for a new job, whether to start a family or not, what clothes to wear, or what to enjoy for supper, there are always a million things that we need to decide on from one day to the next.

Decision-making can be hard, even though we spend a lot of time concentrating and focusing on it each day. Being able to improve our decision-making abilities can often help us learn the best way to make smart decisions for our needs and can make it so much easier to pick what is right for us, whilst saving a ton of time. Some of the techniques that you can use to help improve your decision-making abilities include:

Stop Delaying

Over time, you will find that the simple decisions are the most fun. You can just simply write them on your to-do list and tick them off as you go. When you feel that the stakes increase and you are now faced with making some critical decisions, keep up the same process of getting through things quickly. Never delay just because a decision seems more difficult.

If you struggle with this, then schedule some time to work on the risks, outcomes, and pros and cons that come with your decision. Consider the second and third order effects of your decision, if you can, during this session. Remember that it is always better to make a decision right away. Nothing ever gets done when you sweep the problem under the rug.

Put the Emotions and Ego Away

Decision-making is sometimes difficult because you often let yourself become too invested personally on how this decision is going to make you feel and look. You can still solve the problem in an objective way, but you have to learn how to listen to your logic instead of emotions and ego. One method of doing this is to list out the potential causes and put your emotion and ego on the back burner.

You will be able to make better decisions when you can focus your energy on the facts, rather than looking at any personal deficiencies that may be there.

Always Question the Data You Have

To make informed decisions, you need to ensure that you do a lot of research. You need to find the right information so that you can look through it and get all the points of view before you get started. Another step that you need to take here is to question the data that you receive.

With the rise of the Internet, there is lots of data that you can look up. But that doesn't mean that the information you find is going to be legitimate. Before you decide to use some information to make a decision, you must make sure that you question the data that you have. Check and see if there are any other documents that can support the information that you are working with. Check to see if it matches up with the information that you have already found and if it is unbiased and actually has a good argument associated with it. This helps you to learn whether the information is critical and useful for the decision you are trying to make.

Understand the Risks

The final step and technique to work on here are to plan for all of the risks that can happen with any kind of decision that you decide to make. One way to think about this is to plan for doomsday. Take about ten minutes to look at your problem and then consider the worst-case scenario about any decision that you want to make.

For example, let's say that you need to fire someone from your business. With this technique, you would consider what would be the worst thing that could happen from doing this? There are a lot of ways that you can mitigate the risk of each kind of decision, but you need to take some time to figure out these risks so that you can mitigate the risks and avoid them as much as possible. Try to know the risks from the beginning making the situation easiest to handle as possible.

Chapter 7
Problem-Solving

The next thing that we need to explore is the idea of problem-solving. Problem solving is something that a lot of people struggle with and lack. Some find that their decision-making skills are not always as good as they think they are, and really don't know what to do about it.

The ability to use problem-solving to help you deal with anything that comes your way can be a critical skill that you can utilize on a daily basis. The good news is that anyone can actually learn to improve their problem-solving skills, no matter how bad they currently are. Let's take a look at some of the basics that you should know about problem-solving and how you can go about improving them.

What Is Problem-Solving?

Before we get too far into this chapter, it is important to understand more about this topic. Problem-solving is one of the methods we are going to use to understand what is happening to us in our environment, in identifying the things that we wish to change around us, and to figure out the steps we need to take to get the outcome we desire. Problem-solving is so important; it is the source of all the new inventions that we see around us---the social and cultural evolution---and it can be the basis for market-based economies. When it is used properly, it can be effective at helping with continuous learning, communication, and improvement.

Since problem-solving is so important to many aspects of our daily lives, it is crucial that we learn more about it. Problem-solving is the process of taking observations of what goes on in the environment around us, identifying what you can improve or even change, performing diagnostics on why things are in their current state, developing the alternatives and approaches needed in order to create change, making decisions about which alternative to select out of several, and then taking action to ensure those changes get implemented. And to finish it off, the problem solver will often take the time to observe the impact of those actions to see if they are really successful.

Each step used in problem-solving employs a variety of methods and skills that will help you be more effective to the change that you want, and it can even help you to determine the level of problem complexity that you can address.

Many of us have learned how to solve problems from an early age. We have learnt how to eat, to talk, how to coordinate the movements we do when walking, and even how to communicate. As we progress through our lives, you will work more and more on your problem-solving skills, making them become more refined, matured, and even more sophisticated. This results in us being able to solve problems that are increasingly more difficult.

Problem-solving can be a challenging process, but individuals, as well as companies, will be able to use it in order to exert more control over their environment.

Both business and personal environments are going to be full of processes, interactions, activities, and broken things or at least don't operate in the way that they should. Using the skills that come with problem-solving can give us the tools that we need in order to identify these things, figure out why they don't work properly, and then how we can determine the right action and steps we should take to fix them.

Then, we need to move on to addressing the risks. Humans are adept at learning to find trends, and they can become more aware of any cause and effect relationships that show up in the world around them. These skills can be important because they are used to help us to fix anything that breaks, but they also allow us to make predictions on what is going to happen later on. We are able to do this based on current events and past experiences. The skills that come with problem-solving can be applied to help us anticipate future events and can ensure that we can take action in the present to change future results.

For example, if we know that a machine will often break down at the end of the year, unless we change one of the filters or one of the parts, we may make plans to get that part fixed ahead of time. This helps the machine to keep on working without causing a delay in production or causing a lot of people standing around and not getting things done during work time.

Another thing that problem-solving can help with is to improve performance. Companies and individuals are not going to exist in complete isolation from the rest of the world. There is a complex web of relationships, one that is always changing. As a result of this, the actions that one person uses will often have a direct impact on others in the group, or it could indirectly impact things by changing the dynamics of the environment.

These connections are going to be there no matter what you try to do. And these types of interdependencies enable humans to work together so that they can solve and figure out the more complex problems, while also creating a force that ensures everyone improves their performance and forces them to adapt the improvements that others do. Problem-solving can help us understand the relationships and implement the changes and improvements that are needed to stay competitive and to survive in an environment that is always changing.

And finally, the other thing that problem-solving can help out with is seizing the opportunities. Problem-solving isn't always about responding and fixing the environment that is around us at this moment. It can also be about innovating what there is, creating something that is new and even changing up the environment to make sure it is desirable. Using problem-solving can help us to identify and exploit opportunities that occur in the environment so that we can make predictions and keep control over what is going to happen to us in the future.

As you can see, problem-solving, both its processes and skills, are going to be a very important part of your daily life, whether you are a company or an individual. Developing and then refining these skills through training, learning, and practice can ensure that you are able to solve any problem that you encounter effectively. And with time and practice, you will be able to take on problems that are higher in difficulty and complexity.

Why People Struggle with Problem-Solving

Many people find that they aren't good at problem-solving. Many times, facing problems is going to bring out emotions that we would rather avoid. But being able to solve a problem effectively can be an important skill to help you create the perfect life that you want to have. Avoiding problems simply because you don't like the process of problem-solving just means that any issue you are dealing with could get worse.

You will find that, many times, those who are more emotionally sensitive are the ones who are the most creative when it comes to problem-solving. This is usually because they want to avoid the issues that come with those emotions, so they will often look for solutions that others may not even consider or think about.

But there are also people who seem to have trouble with problem-solving no matter what. This may be due to their natural problem-solving ability being damaged by various life situations, which may have caused them to develop a type of fear any time that they run into some kind of problem they need to solve.

Going back to those who are more emotionally sensitive, problem-solving can be stifled when they receive feedback. For these particular types of individuals, when it comes to receiving feedback from those whom they love, it will often hit them hard emotionally. If you have had issues with people in the past criticizing your problem-solving skills or criticizing the ideas you might have had for others, you may have been made to feel disheartened and put off offering suggestions or ever putting any of your problem-solving ideas into action.

So, even though these emotionally sensitive people are more likely to come up with creative solutions to their problems, more than often they will come unstuck when it comes to problem-solving because they worry too much about what other people may think of them and their ideas. If they can learn to care less about what others think and not let them be influenced by this, their problem-solving skills would become a lot more effective as a result.

You may also find that your own emotions, whether you are emotionally sensitive or not, can be an issue with your problem-solving skills. If your always saying things like "I don't know what to do" because you have the fear that your sibling is going to be upset with you, then the biggest issue you are dealing with here is that you don't want to handle the emotions that come with the best solution.

Emotions are not always a bad thing. These emotions can sometimes give you helpful information that you can consider, but for most of the time we become victims of our emotions which lead us into not living a life we really want. Picking a choice because you are scared of how the other person will react, avoiding something because it makes you sad, or having an unjustified fear that you won't be able to pass a test can be examples of your emotions getting in the way of you choosing the best solution. No matter what problems you are dealing with, you always need to consider what emotions are at play and make sure that they don't get in the way of the best solution.

Over time, you may consider that you cannot always manage the emotions that you have when you feel unsure about the way you react to any kind of situation, or that you cannot predict the way that certain emotions may affect the behavior that you exhibit. If so, you are more likely to avoid any new ideas and situations. This drives us to stick with the familiar, not because it is the best, but because it is the familiar and what we are used to.

You may also have had a problem where you have received feedback accusing you of being wrong in the way that you feel or think. This can happen often to those who are emotionally sensitive. For these people, especially if the feedback they receive tells them they are always wrong, it is easy to look to others to help determine how realistic or valuable your ideas are. In some cases, you may even start to depend on others to help you figure out all your problems because your now led to believe that you can't do this on your own. Basically, what you have learnt in all of this is to just be passive.

If you have tried to work on problem-solving in the past, but all its does is cause you bigger problems, or you find that others chastise you for your efforts, you start to believe that you cannot solve a problem on your own because you will always be wrong. You will start to spend your time seeing who will solve your problems for you. Your usual reactions to a problem may be something like "Tell me what to do, just tell me what to do" or "I don't know what to do".

If any of these descriptions tend to describe you, then there is still things you can do to help. Problem-solving is a skill and a process that you can learn. The first step that you must work on is figuring out how to regulate your emotions so that you can think clearly and use coping skills that are the most effective for your needs.

Everyone can learn how to work on their problem-solving skills, they may just need to learn how to avoid the emotions more or at least limit them as much as possible, and learn that they can actually handle their own problems without having to rely on anyone else.

The Process of Problem-Solving

The process of problem-solving is a mental process that involves discovering, analyzing, and then solving a variety of problems. You will usually just work on one problem at a time, but sometimes, there may be a few problems that relate to each other that you can work on together at the same time. The end goal with problem-solving is to overcome any obstacles that you are facing so you can find a solution that will help resolve the issue.

Choosing the best strategy that you should use for solving any problem is often going to depend on the situation. In some situations, people see that learning everything they can about an issue or problem using this knowledge to come up with a solution is the best option. In other cases, it is better to try and get an insight or use creativity to come up with the best solution.

Now, there are a few steps that you can take when it comes down to problem-solving. Regardless of the different problems that you may be faced with, the process for problem-solving is the same each time. To solve any problem that you encounter correctly, it is important that you follow a series of steps. These steps are often known as the problem-solving cycle, which will include coming up with the right strategies for a solution and how to organize your knowledge.

While this is a cycle portrayed sequentially, there can be a lot of variations and movements in the way people go about following these steps. Instead, we will more than often skip these steps or go through the same steps a few times until the right solution is reached. Some of the steps that are shown in the problem-solving cycle include:

The first step is to identify the problem. While this is a step that may seem pretty obvious, you may find that identifying the problem is sometimes more complicated than it seems. In some cases, you may make the mistake when identifying the wrong source of the problem, doing this will just make any attempts you use to solve the problem useless and inefficient. Finding the right problem and the source of that problem can help put you on the right path.

The next step that you should work on is defining your problem. Once you can identify your problem or the issue that you should work on, it is time to define the problem. If you have a full definition of the problem that you are working on, then you will be able to solve it a lot quicker.

Now, we need to work on forming our strategy. It is important for you to come up with a good and effective strategy that will help you to solve the problem. The approach that you will use can depend on your own personal preferences as well as the situation that you are trying to work on. During this time, you will also need to organize the information you will use for your strategy. Before you can come up with a good solution, you first need to organize all of the available information. Think about what you know concerning the problem and even the things that you don't know. The more information that you can gather, the easier it is to prepare and come up with a good solution.

Another thing that you can work on is allocating the resources that you have. No one has an unlimited amount of time, money, and resources in order to solve any problem, no matter how important that problem is. before you even get started with solving this problem, you must determine how important and urgent this problem is. If you find that it is really important, you will want to allocate extra resources. If it is something that you need to work on but is not a high priority, then you can allocate your resources a bit differently.

At this point, you should have a good solution in place. Whether you figured out the right solution on your own or with the help of others, you should have explored a few different possibilities in order to help. Now, it is time to monitor your progress. Those who are effective at problem-solving will make sure that they monitor their progress while they work towards their solution. If you find that you aren't making any progress towards your goal, then you might need to relook at the whole strategy and see if you need to change your approach.

And finally, it is always useful to evaluate the results you get. After you pick out your solution and have implemented, it is important to take some time to evaluate the results. This helps you to figure out if the solution you chose was the right one for this problem. Sometimes, the evaluation is right away, and other times you may wait until the solution has some time to work before doing the evaluation.

Problem-Solving in the Workplace and in Life

In addition to working with problem-solving in your own personal life, there may be times when you need to work on your problem-solving skills in your workplace. Sometimes, this can just be things like finishing up a project efficiently and on time, and in other cases these skills need to be used in order to help avoid a crisis. Being able to recognize the various examples of problem-solving in the workplace can help you prepare more for work-related issues. Let's look at a few examples of how this can work as well as some of the techniques that you can use for you to do well with problem-solving in the workplace.

Brainstorming

You will find that there are many instances where the workplace can benefit from new ideas of the team. And to come up with these new ideas, you will need to work on brainstorming. Everyone on the team, from the staff to the management, would need to come into the room. They can have a piece of paper to start. Then, given a time limit, they should start to write down any idea that comes into their mind. There are no bad answers here, just have them write down whatever they think about because no one else will see the paper if they don't want to share it.

After everyone has a chance to write down their ideas, the group will share these ideas and then expand on what they see as the best ideas until they come up with the basis of their solution. Make sure that everyone on the team and everyone in the room has a chance to share their ideas to help with the creativity. Brainstorming can be a great way for you to get input from many different people, providing you with more solutions to help you succeed.

Delegation

Each person in the group will need to work with their own set of responsibilities. The responsibilities that they get will be based on the educational background and experience that each person has. There should never be the issue with one person taking on all of the work that comes with a project. Once a solution is figured out, you can take some time to discuss the different tasks to complete that solution, and then determine who will be in charge of each part. Make sure that the meeting doesn't end without everyone knowing what job and task they need to work on.

Committees

You may find that working with a committee can work either in a permanent or, sometimes, temporary position. The committee can be a workgroup responsible for handling specific issues in the workplace. For example, if your department for logistics runs into some challenges with one of your shipping companies, then it may be possible to create a committee that helps you to look into what this issue is and what is causing it before coming up with the proper solution.

It is pretty common for these committees to include employees with specific skills which are needed to get the job done. The committee that you use to deal with the shipping issue above will probably include a representative that works with the problem company, one that works with a better shipping company, and the shipping manager since these individuals know how to handle these kinds of situations.

Evaluations

During problem-solving, evaluations on a regular basis are always important. Taking the time to monitor department progress and employee progress versus the goals of the company is a constant problem-solving process in the workplace, and it is very important when you want to maintain productivity. These evaluations can be used by managers to help compare actual performance against any of the goals that are found in the business plan of a company or maybe in their marketing plan.

The analysis of these results can be used in order to get a good idea of the issues that should be addressed, and then the team or the management can use this to create the perfect plan to address the issues. Let's say that the revenue of a business is falling and it is lower than the projections of the company for the year. There would then be an evaluation done on the company's sales process to reveal any shortcomings that may show up in the sales methods that should be corrected in order to get the revenue on track to where it should be.

Useful Problem-Solving Skills and How to Develop Them

When it comes to problem-solving, there are actually a few key skills that you need to work on in order to make it easier to solve any problem you encounter. Some of the skills that you need when learning to develop better problem-solving skills include:

1. **Creativity:** Most of the time a problem is going to be solved either systematically or intuitively. Intuition can be used when you don't need to find any new knowledge. You already have the information that you need to make a quick decision and solve the problem, or you can at least use your experience or your common sense to do so. Sometimes, problems that are more complex or that you have never worked on before will need a more systematic approach, and this will often need some creative thinking to help you out.
2. **Researching Skills**: Being able to define and solve any problem that you have can often require you to research. Sometimes, the research is simple, and you can just get away

with a quick search on Google. But there are also times when the research project will be more in-depth and rigorous to find the answers that you need.

3. **Teamworking:** You will find that many problems are going to be defined and solved the best when you get input from others. Teamworking may just sound like something that you do at work, but you will find that it can be important at school and at home as well. If you cannot work in a team, then it may be time to work on this in order to help with your critical thinking.

4. **Emotional Intelligence:** Emotional intelligence is very important when it comes to becoming a critical thinker. The emotional intelligence that you have, as well as the ability to recognize the emotions of others, will help you to guide you to an appropriate solution. If you can solve a problem in the right manner, without worrying about emotions getting in the way, then you will find things can be much easier to decide.

5. **Risk Management:** Solving a variety of problems will always involve a certain amount

of risk. You always need to weigh the risk against the idea of not solving a problem ahead of time.

6. **Decision-Making:** Decision-making and problem-solving are often closely related. And being able to make a decision can be very important when it comes to finding various options and alternatives. You need to be able to research and figure out the best solution based on the information that you are given.

Techniques to Develop Your Problem-Solving Abilities

Now that we have taken some time to discuss problem-solving and some of the skills that are needed to help with this, it is time to work on the best techniques needed to develop these abilities. There are many different techniques that can help, but we are going to look at the top six effective ways to enhance your problem-solving skills to help you get started.

Focus Less on the Problem and More on the Solution

Studies have been proven that the brain cannot find solutions if you focus all of your energy on a problem.

The reason for this is that when you focus just on a problem, you are just feeding the brain negativity. This will just cause you to build up negative emotions which will hinder your thinking ability.

This doesn't mean that you get to ignore the problem you are dealing with. But don't let it bother you to the extent where you're getting stressed out. Instead, try to think about it calmly so you don't start the spiral that we have just mentioned. It can help out in many cases to acknowledge the problem first, and then, while remaining calm, move the focus to more of a solution-oriented mindset where you keep fixed on the possible solution, rather than focusing on what went wrong or who might be at fault.

Adapt the Five Why's

The five why's can be very helpful no matter what kind of problem you are dealing with, you may have heard about them being used before in business and other situations. This requires you to ask why about a problem at least five times. The more that you can ask this question, the closer you will get to the proper solution. You don't have to limit yourself to five times, but it is known as the five why's to encourage you to ask why at least this amount of times.

When you repeatedly ask yourself the question of why on one problem, then you can dig deeper into the root cause of a problem. You may find a ton of solutions for a problem, but if you don't discover the root of that problem, then it's likely that you are not finding the proper solution for your needs.

Let's look at an example of how this can work. Let's say, our problem is that we always show up late for work. The way that you can implement the five why's with this includes:

1. Why am I late to work? I always hear the alarm and click on the snooze button so that I can go back to sleep.
2. Why do I want to keep on sleeping in the morning? I still feel tired when it is time to wake up.
3. Why do I feel tired in the morning? I stayed up too late the night before so I am now tired.
4. Why did I go to bed late the night before? I didn't feel too sleepy at bedtime, but that was probably because I was drinking coffee. I also

spent a lot of time scrolling on Facebook or another social media site and couldn't stop.
5. Why did I decide to drink the coffee? Because I felt really sleepy the day before and had trouble staying awake at work, so I drank the coffee.

With this option, you can see that you have the solution and have put yourself into a vicious cycle here. If you didn't go that far to find the root of the problem, you may have decided to just set a few more alarms and then been up every five minutes in the morning. You can instead stop surfing endlessly on Facebook at night so that you can get to bed, feel more energetic during the day, and don't need to rely on the coffee that keeps you awake.

Simplify as Much as Possible

Even though simplicity is the best, we often have a tendency to over complicate things. If you are working on a problem and can't seem to come up with the right solution, then it maybe time to try to simplify your approach.

Take a look at the problem and try to remove as many details as possible, bringing yourself back to the basics.

Try looking for a really easy and obvious solution. And this can lead you to be surprised by the results. You already know that the simple things are the most productive, and this can be true with your problem as well.

List out as Many of the Solutions as you Can

When you are problem-solving, make sure that you entertain all of the solutions that you can find. Even if you think that the solution seems a little silly at first, you need to keep an open mind about everything. Even if you don't end up using a particular solution, you may find that it is the springboard you need to trigger the solution you pick.

During this stage, make sure that you keep your mind open and never ridicule yourself when the solution may seem stupid. The crazy and silly ideas are the ones that often trigger the more viable and better solutions that you end up choosing.

Think Laterally

Sometimes, the best way to come up with the solution to your problem is to think laterally. For this one, consider the saying "You can't dig a hole in a different place by digging it deeper." What this means is that you should work to change your approach and see if you can look at it in a new way.

You can flip the objective around and see if there is some kind of solution to the problem, even if that solution is the polar opposite of where you were looking.

Use Language That Opens up New Doors

Another solution that you can work with is using the right kind of language. Often, our language, whether we speak it out loud or in our heads, is negative and can make it harder to come up with the solution that we need. You should always lead your thinking with some phrases like "what if" and "imagine if". These terms can open up the brains ability to think more so that we can think in a more creative way which will encourage better solutions. Make sure you avoid negative and closed language like "This is not right, but" or "I don't think" because this will only limit your way of thinking.

Problem-solving can be difficult. You will always want to try and come up with the best solution for the situation that you are in, but you may be limited to the options that you can be or the solutions you can find. Using the tips and techniques in this chapter can help you find the perfect solution, no matter what.

Conclusion

Thanks for making it through to the end of the book. We hope it was informative and able to provide you with all of the tools you need to achieve your goals whatever they may be.

The next step is to begin using the critical thinking skills that we have discussed in this guide to help you make more informed decisions throughout your life. While critical thinking doesn't have to be used all the time, you will find that there are many scenarios and situations in our lives when we could definitely think more critically to get better results.

This guide has spent some time looking at the basics of critical thinking and how it can be used to improve your own life. By the time you are done, you will have a better understanding of what this skill is about and why it is so important for you to use. You will also know the best times to utilize critical thinking to get the best results in your life as possible.

Memory improvement Mastery

By Dale Owen.

Introduction

In the following chapters we will discuss everything that you need to know in order to improve your memories ability to remember things such as dates, people, events, and other important things that go on in our daily lives. All of us struggle with our memory on occasion. We often forget things like where our keys are, or where we have left our wallet when it's time to leave the house. We sometimes even overschedule ourselves due to forgetting things like a particular event that is due to happen in our lives. Failing to remember things often can usually lead to upsetting people, causing ourselves to feel let down as a result.

Having a lapse in memory on the odd occasion is normal. Sometimes we aren't able to encode the information in the way that we should, or we just aren't focusing on the information enough because we are often busy and occupied by other things. However, when these things start to happen on a more regular basis, then we can expect problems to occur. When these types of problems arise, it is natural and perfectly normal to start looking for easy ways that we can use to improve our memory.

In this guide we are going to spend some time talking about how the memory works and the different ways that you can improve your memory. First, we will start out by trying to get an understanding of how the mind actually works. We will talk about why we forget certain things, why some people are better at remembering than others, and even how age is going to affect the way that the memory works. From there, we will do a discussion on what will cause most memory problems and what we are able to do to improve these problems so that they don't start to cause more issues or get worse further down the line.

Then, we are going to move onto some of the various techniques that you can use to help improve your memory and ensure its functioning as optimal as possible. We will then finish off with information on simple things that you can implement into your daily life to improve your memory as well as some basics to help reboot and recharge the mind any time that you need.

All of us want to improve our memory and ensure that it works in the best way possible. There are a variety of tools and techniques that we can use to make this happen.

Chapter 1
Understanding How the Mind Works

The mind has long been thought of as a mysterious thing. There is a lot that we still don't know when it comes to the brain. We don't fully understand how it stores memories—even though we are finding out that a lot of facts out there are wrong and that there isn't just one place in the brain that holds onto these memories.

Being able to understand how the mind works and how we form and store memories can be critical when it comes to ensuring that we get the most out of improving our memory. This chapter is going to take some time to discuss the different ways the mind works, how we are able to memorize things, how memories are formed, why some people can remember better than others, how aging can affect the way that we remember things, and even a discussion on photographic memory to help us get started.

The Brain and How It Works to Memorize Things

The more that you are able to learn about the memory, the better that you are going to be able to understand the best way to improve your own memory. Most of us are going to talk about memory like it is something that we have—like lots of hair or bad eyes. However, the memory isn't going to exist in the same way that a part of our body exists simply because it's not something that we are able to touch. Instead, memory is a concept that refers to the process of remembering.

There has been a lot of research done to discuss the memory and how it works. In the past, there were many experts who found it easiest to describe the memory like a filing cabinet that had different folders for each memory, and that is how all the memories were stored. Other experts would say its like a supercomputer in the brain that would hold these memories.

However, today, many researchers believe that the memory for humans can be even more elusive and complex than was thought possible in the past. In fact, our memories aren't even stored in one particular part of the brain over another. The memories are going to be stored all across the brain, which can make this system even more complex to deal with.

To start this section out, let's think back to what you had for breakfast this morning. If you had an image of eggs and bacon, or maybe some cereal shows up, this doesn't mean that you dredged it up from some neural alleyway. What really happened was that this memory showed up because it was a result of an incredibly complex constructive power, something that all of us are able to do, that reassembled the memory impressions from a web-like pattern of cells that aren't found in just one area of the brain but throughout all the different parts.

In fact, what we know of the memory right now is it's just a group of systems that come together in order to create, store, and recall our memories. When the brain is able to process this information normally, all of these systems are going to work together in order to provide us with some cohesive thoughts. Because of this, what may seem like a single memory to us is very complex.

Let's say that you are thinking about some kind of object. For this, we are going to think about a pen. Your brain is then going to retrieve the name of the object, the shape it is, the function, and even the sounds that the pen can make when it writes on the page. Each part of the memory of the pen is going to show up from different regions of the brain, this also comes from different areas to form the whole picture. It is only recently that neurologists are starting to understand the different ways that these memories are being reassembled when we call them up.

When you are looking to remember something, you will need to go to the unconscious level of the brain and retrieve the information so it comes back to the conscious mind. While most people believe that they have either a good or bad memory, most people have strengths and weaknesses when it comes to what they can and can't remember. If you do have some troubles with remembering a certain topic, unless you have other diseases or factors at play, this usually is not indicative of the whole system of the memory not working.

Let's look at an example here. We want to try to remember where we put our eyeglasses. When you head to bed at night, you need to register where your put your glasses. You need to focus and pay attention to whereabouts you have set them on the bedside table before bed. You then need to also have awareness of where you are putting them, or it is impossible to remember this location the next morning. Next, all of this information is retained, and ready for you to retrieve it, later on. If your memory and the system with it is working properly, then when it is time to wake up the next morning, you will know the exact spot where you left the glasses.

Now, if you woke up the next morning and you forgot where your glasses are, then there are a few different things that may have happened, including:

1. You may not have really registered where you placed those glasses in the first place.
2. You may have had trouble retaining the information that you just registered.
3. You may be struggling to retrieve the memory in an accurate manner.

What this means is that if you want to stop forgetting the location of your eyeglasses, then you need to make sure that each of these stages of the remembering process is working as it should be. If you have forgotten something, it is likely that you weren't able to encode it effectively. Often this happens because you became distracted while the encoding process took place. When you forget where you place the glasses, this can be a sign that the location of the glasses didn't end up in the memory to start with.

Distractions that show up when you try to remember something new can sometimes get in the way of helping the brain encode the memories. If something isn't encoded, then you won't be able to encode it later on. If you have ever taken the time to remember something once, and you weren't able to, but then you could remember that item later on, this is a sign that there was a mismatch between your retrieval cues and the encoding of the information you wanted to remember.

The Flaws of the Brain and the Mind

Our brains and minds can be marvelous things. They help us in our daily functioning, completing unfinished work, getting us to and from places, making decisions, and so much more. Our minds help us to store memories and learn something new almost every day. But there are some limitations that come into play as well.

There are so many stimuli that come at us from every direction all day long. From sounds, sights, smells to things we touch and everything in between. If our brains even tried to take in all of this, we would be overwhelmed and wouldn't be able to get anything done at all. Because of this, our minds have to adjust and learn what is important and what isn't as important, turning off everything else to ensure that we are able to just take in what is the most important.

Now, often the brain is going to take over and do this automatically for us. As we go along our day, we find that we are able to just get things done without thinking about it at all. For example, when we head into work, how much do you really notice along the way? Do you recognize all the cars that pass you, what music is on the radio, or anything else other than the route you are taking? There is a ton of stuff that you pass on a drive to work, this is often the same when it comes to other tasks that you do. But unless something out of the normal happens, like an accident that delays and makes you late to work, it is likely you will just go to work and not think anything more about it.

You can learn how to focus on the things that you want to remember. Going back to the example of the ride to work, the next time you head out, move your focus onto the drive, taking in everything and seeing it as important. This will open your mind and your eyes to things that you never saw in the past, and allow you to train the mind into memorizing things that you usually wouldn't have.

The brain can sometimes be distorted by our emotions, both when you are experiencing the event and later on when the memory comes back out in the recall. With the first instance, you may find that your brain will distort some things based on the mood. For example, if you were feeling elated because of something, you may have a memory of a great day at work or a fantastic drive through traffic, even if these weren't that great of things.

When your memories get distorted based on your current mood, this often leads you to think about situations and things based on that particular mood. For example, if your current mood is that your sad and depressed, then you may run into the issue of only being able to remember the bad stuff and sadness that our memory lets us think about.

Our brain is a powerful tool. We are able to control it, but since there is just so much going on in our lives and around us, it is sometimes hard to get it to make and store memories in the correct manner. Learning how to control the mind and to get the most out of it can really make a big difference when it comes to how well we are able to store our own memories and remember things later on.

Memory Consolidation

Memory consolidation is going to be a process that is needed in coding memory so that you can retrieve it later on. Without this consolidation process, there isn't any way for you to store information in your brain, which is something that needs to happen if you want to form and store memories to use later on. Consolidation is something that you can observe in many species of animals, and each one seems to have a different capacity for forming and storing these new memories. There are several things that are able to interfere with the consolidation of memories.

The process of memory consolidation is going to begin within a few minutes on the synaptic level whenever the brain encounters something new, whether it is new or not, and then takes the time to interact with it. System consolidation is going to happen in the long term, usually over weeks and months when the brain works to develop new pathways so it is easier to access that memory. The stronger these pathways are, the easier it is for you to recall them later on.

Research that has been done on the brain shows how memories aren't just stored in one particular part of the brain, but they are spread out in various locations. Consolidation is the process of making these spread out memories more accessible, basically creating a good index or map to the brain to ensure that you are able to retrieve any of the memories that are needed when you need them most.

Once your brain has gone through and stored a memory, it can recall that memory at any time you want. Initially, it was believed that memories were stored there permanently. But in recent years, researchers have learned that these memories need to be reconsolidated every time that you call them out.

Memories can become labile. What this means is that the memories are fragile and it is possible for you to disrupt them any time you recall them. The process of reconsolidation returns these recalled memories back to the right place in the brain so that you are able to use them again.

There are a few different functions that can come into play when we talk about memory consolidation. First off, the hippocampus is often going to play a very important role when it comes to forming memories and then storing them. Other parts of the brain will help out as well, based on the type of memory that is involved in the process.

For example, REM sleep, or rapid eye movement, can come into play when it is time for the consolidation of memories. This may show that this process happens when we spend time sleeping and refreshing the brain. Without proper amounts of sleep, it may be difficult for you to consolidate the memories in the proper manner. If you are suffering with the issue of remembering things and holding memories for the long-term, it may be time for you to consider changing your sleeping patterns so you can see better results with your memory.

Another thing to look at is some of the phenomena that researchers have been able to observe when you learn. While this process of consolidation is normally going to take a longer period of time, there are studies of people who were involved in learning tasks have shown that the brain does have the power to consolidate a memory successfully in an hour or less in certain cases.

The methods that are used in order to present the information can make a big difference in how long that process takes—and the number of times you repeat the information can help as well. Repeating the same information to yourself over and over can cause some synaptic changes that will then lead to rapid consolidation of memory. This could help show why recitation can help you to learn and keep things in your memory for a long period of time.

Why and How We Forget and Remember Certain Things

One of the normal functions of emotion is to help enhance certain memories so that we are able to recall these experiences, especially when they have more relevance or importance for our survival. These emotions are going to be similar to what we do with a highlighter pen. They will go through and emphasize certain aspects of experiences to make these more memorable for us. Memory formation is going to involve the registering of information, processing and storing that information, and then retrieving it later on.

Emotion is going to help affect all of the phases of memory formation. We are able to remember things better when there is some kind of strong emotion tied to it. This is why we are better able to remember our wedding day or the birth of a child or our graduation but have a hard time remembering where we put the keys. The keys have no emotions tied to them, but the other events do. Let's take a look at the way that emotion can affect the formation of memory:

Attention

First, we need to look at the attention that we give an event. Attention is going to help guide our focus to select what is the most relevant to our lives, and often it is going to be associated with novelty. Nothing is going to move our focus over to a certain event like a surprise, for example.

Think of it this way. While we may find that we enjoy a particular conversation one time, if we went back through and had the exact same conversation a second time, we would find it to be bull. The emotional intensity is going to act as a way to narrow the scope of our attention so that a few objects can be emphasized, while the rest are ignored or not focused on. Since we are not able to focus on everything that happens in our whole lives, being able to focus on a very narrow area allows for optimal use of the limited attention that we have.

Consolidating the Memory

Most of the information that we are able to acquire is going to be forgotten and it never makes it on the long journey to becoming a long-term memory. There is just too much for us to try and remember on a day to day basis, that it doesn't make sense to try and fit it all into the long-term memory. When we start to learn a problem that is complex, our short-term memory will open up, like an automatic action that happens for us. But then, how does the brain decide which of the memories in the short-term memory get erased and which ones get to move into more permanent storage?

Events and memories that have some kind of emotion behind them, especially really strong emotions, are the ones that are going to be more likely to get stored in the long-term memory. The stress hormones of cortisol and epinephrine are there to enhance your memory, which ables it to consolidate the contents of that memory. When we look at this in an evolutionary way, it makes logical sense for us to imprint dangerous situations with some extra clarity because this allows us to avoid some of the harmful stuff or the things that causes us stress and other issues, and then avoid those situations later.

Memory Recall

Memories of experiences that are painful and emotional are going to linger much longer than those that would cause us actual physical pain. Contrary to what we learned in the past about sticks and stones may break our bones, but words never hurt us, evidence shows that feelings being hurt can be much worse than any physical pain. We never seem to forget how we made them feel.

What is really interesting here when it comes to our emotions and memories is that some common pain killers, such as acetaminophen found in Tylenol, may not only be effective when it comes to physical pain that we feel, like sore muscles and headaches, it can also be effective with emotional pain.

Priming

Past memories are often going to be triggered, also known as primed, by the environment that you are in. Priming refers to activating behavior through the power of unconscious suggestion. There has been previous research that shows how people who were made to think of self—discipline (they had to work on unscrambling sentences about this topic), were immediately able to make more future oriented snack choices compared to those who were given the same exercise, but on self-indulgence.

In the case above, the goal stored in the long-term memory was retrieved and then put into our working or short-term memory. The way that we bring these out and influence the results that we get over time. This is similar to the idea of going into the library and automatically talking in a quiet voice, because that we was taught from an early age what we should do when visiting libraries.

Mood Memory

The emotional state that we are in at that current moment can really facilitate the recall of experiences that may have had a similar emotional tone for us. So, if we are in a good or happy mood, we are more likely to recall happy and pleasant events. If we are in an angry or sad mood, then these are the kinds of memories we are going to recall.

For example, you may be more likely to recall some positive experiences in your childhood if you are currently in a good mood. But when you are in a bad mood, you are more primed to think about negative thoughts and emotions. Changing yourself from one mood to the other and changing up the memories that you have at that time can sometimes be a challenge for people.

Blanking Out

You may find that high levels of stress can lead to issues with a memory deficit. This is why it is a common experience to blank out mentally when you have a very high pressure situation, like a test or an interview, going on at that time. Many times we struggle with remembering anything when we are stressed out and dealing with a lot of different things on our plate.

For the most part, anxiety can influence the way that our brains function in what is known as an inverted U-curve, or a curvilinear manner. This is a phenomenon that is known as the Yerkes-Dodson law. What this basically means is that when levels of arousal are too low, such as when we are bored, and when these levels of arousal tend to be too high, such as when we are dealing with fear or anxiety, our performance is more likely to suffer as a result.

When we are in situations of boredom or otherwise not being aroused mentally, the mind becomes very unfocused and doesn't know how to proceed. But when we are in situations that are overly stimulated and too hard to handle, the focus of our attention is going to be too narrow, and this can cause us to lose out on a lot of the information. Having a moderate amount of arousal is necessary to ensure that we aren't bored and unfocused, but that we can still catch the details that we need that are around us.

Duration Neglect

Another thing to consider is the duration neglect. The method that we use to remember events isn't always going to be made up of a total of every individual moment. Instead, most people find that they are going to remember and overemphasize the peak moment, the worst moment, the best moments, and the last moment. In the process, they are going to neglect the duration of the experience as a whole.

This is why we may have a great time at a party, but then one small thing at the end can ruin the whole experience. Think back to your last vacation. If it lasted for a week or more, there is going to be a lot of information to keep track of and too much for you to reasonably evaluate to tell if it is enjoyable. So, you would use the duration neglect, also known as the peak end rule, to help you heavily way the best moments of the trip with the most recent moment of that trip, to help you come up with an evaluation.

So basically, what this means is that we are going to rely heavily on our own emotions to tell us whether we will need to remember something or not. The more that a memory is tied to a specific emotion, especially a strong one like happiness, sadness, and anger, the more likely we are to remember it.

Why Some People Remember More Than Others

Every person is going to have a different kind of memory. This is going to depend on a number of factors, including your genetics, your age, and how much you stimulate and work on the mind. If you can work and keep yourself healthy and doing well, and you work to regularly challenge your brain, then you will find that it is easier to remember things compared to others.

First, we need to look at age. For some people, aging can cause their memories to go down a little. If you make sure to challenge yourself on a regular basis, get outside and move around, do some mental challenges on occasion, and eat a healthy diet, then the memory loss is not going to be that big of a deal. In fact, healthy adults can easily keep their memory as sharp as it was when they were younger, no matter how old they are.

For some people, it is all about genetics. If you have a family history of dementia and Alzheimer's, then you may find that your more prone to memory decline more than other people. This doesn't mean that all is lost and you are never going to be able to keep your brain and your mind sharp. It just means that you may need more mental practice and more challenges to keep the brain working well. Even then, you may not be able to get the memory up to what other people can do. But you do still have some control, so don't just sit back and let the deterioration occur over time just because you think it is inevitable that your memory will be gone.

Finally, you can always work on stimulating the brain and making it work harder. The biggest reason that the memory starts to fade is that the brain is not getting the workout that it needs. We assume that the brain will just stay strong and smart without any work on our part. But if we never work the brain by doing something new, or we never focus on going somewhere new, learning something new, or providing a challenge for the brain, then we are just going to end up with memory issues.

There are a lot of different ways that you can make sure your brain gets stronger and that, despite age and other factors, you won't end up losing your memory. You can work on mind puzzles and games. You can go out and explore some new places and meet new people, even traveling to help open up the mind. You can learn a new language or something else that has always interested you to help your mind stay sharp.

Some of the people who have better memories have this because they actively work on it. They may employ various memory and thinking techniques on a regular basis. They may spend more time reading and enjoying the arts, and may get out and explore new places and see new things. They also keep their environment stimulating, rather than just sitting around watching television all day. Some of the other factors can come into play on occasion, but we do have a bit of control when it comes to how well our brains and memories can function. If we are proactive, we are more likely to see that our memories actually improve and we will see some amazing results that others are jealous of as well.

What About Photographic Memories

One thing that we need to take some time to consider here is the idea of photographic memory. This kind of memory is quite a bit different from what we are used to when we talk about the memory. While most of us struggle to remember lists or other information for a very long time, people with a photographic memory can often remember things years down the line, and they will remember it perfectly no matter how long has passed.

A person who has a photographic memory is someone who is able to remember events and scenes as detailed and precise images. There have been a lot of studies that suggest that having a truly photographic memory is pretty much non-existence. But there are people who have what is known as an eidetic memory. This is similar, but a little bit different. These two terms are very similar though and most of the people you meet who have really strong memories will fit into the category of eidetic memory.

For those who believe that there is a photographic memory and that some people do have such a thing, it is thought that these people are able to store information, usually in the form of a detailed image, and then that person can pull it out and recall what happened at will. For example, this kind of memory would allow someone to describe a painting in detail after just seeing it one time, or they may be able to recite out whole passages from a book that they had just glanced at.

Now, some people are believed to be able to work hard and gain the skills. There are different techniques that can be utilized in order to make this a technique that works well for you. But this means that you have to develop the skill, not that it is one you are born with.

On the other hand, there are those who have an eidetic memory. These individuals are going to store visual information with a very high level of precision. This allows them to repeat information with a ton of details, but they can usually only do this for a short period of time after they see the material. So, if they just saw a painting briefly, they may be able to describe it with a lot of detail. But they wouldn't be able to do the same thing down the line.

Eidetic memory can be found in almost anyone, but it is the most common in children, and it often fades with age. The reason for this, or at least the reason that most researchers think that this happens, is because most children are going to store the information they encounter in a visual way, unlike adults who focus more on the verbal.

For those individuals who have more of an eidetic memory, whether it is from children or adults, they appear to store the information in ways that are very different fundamentally, from the way that we will store memories. This allows them to have a better chance of recalling the information later on. This type of memory is not going to be the same as a photographic memory, a word that we hear a lot but doesn't really happen, but they may appear as similar to the outsider.

There has been a lot of people throughout history who have been able to demonstrate an astounding ability to memorize things, whether it was the lines of many plays, to the details of visual scenes. These individuals may seem like they had a photographic memory, but in reality, it is more likely that they spent years training themselves to remember things like this.

For those who work in various fields were memory is a key to their success, such as with musicians, painters, and actors, there are many different memory tricks can help make things easier. These individuals may do a better job of remembering things and utilizing those tricks, but often it is more through hard work and some dedication, and not memory magic like we may think.

This is good news for most people though. It means that we can also learn to make our memories sharper and to ensure that we are going to be able to bring back information at any time that it is needed. You don't have to feel bad because you don't have a photographic memory. You don't have to let things slide just because you are getting older. You can still utilize these same techniques and tricks to help make strengthen your brain power.

How Age Can Affect the Memory

There have been many studies done to look at the effects of aging on our memories. Many people claim that they have a hard time remembering things when they age and feel like there isn't much that they can do to stop this progression and help them out. While some people do experience issues with dementia, Alzheimer's and other types of memory loss as they age, the normal healthy person may not have to worry about aging as much when it comes to your memory and how strong it is.

Yes, many times you may notice that you forget the keys or why you walked into a room, and remembering names starts to become more and more difficult. But this doesn't mean that our memories have to fade and that it is only a matter of time before we can remember anything. No matter what our age is, we are able to still remember things and keep our memory sharp.

Researchers have a few different theories when it comes to what's behind the mind deterioration that can happen when you start to age, but most suspect that as we age, this causes major cell loss in a tiny region found in the front of the brain that can lead to a drop in the production of a neurotransmitter known as acetylcholine. This transmitter is very important when it comes to your memory and to learning overall.

In addition, a few of the parts of the brain that you need and are essential to your memory can be very vulnerable when it comes to aging. One area, which is the hippocampus, is going to start losing about 5 percent of all its nerve cells with each decade that passes. This means that you could potentially lose about 20 percent of these nerve cells by the time you get to your 80s unless you are careful and work to preserve them. In addition, it is thought that the brain itself, without the proper exercises, can start shrinking and becoming less efficient as you age as well.

These are natural things that can occur to your brain as you age. There are also other things that you could do that may speed up the decline. For example, if you have a genetic predisposition to memory problems or other brain diseases, then this can make things worse. If you were ever exposed to poisons this can cause problems. Also things like drinking and smoking can play a big part in causing your memory to lose function. Each of these things, plus more, can all speed up the decline of your memory.

As you age, there are also some physical changes that make the brain not work as efficiently as before and this makes it hard for you to remember in an efficient manner. However, this doesn't mean that losing your memory and ending up with dementia is something that you just have to prepare for and have no say in the matter. In fact, while there are some abilities that do tend to decline with age, overall memory can still remain strong for most people, even when they progress though their 70s.

Research has already shown us that the average 70-year-old is going to be able to perform just as well on certain cognitive tests as their 20-year-old counterparts. It has been found that those in their 60s and 70s are able to do much better with the verbal intelligence than younger people. Studies have also shown that many of the memory problems that some older people deal with can be lessened, and in some cases reversed.

In one of these studies, nursing home populations were studied. This found that patients were actually able to make large improvements with their memory when they were given rewards and challenges along the way. Mental stimulation and physical exercise can also work to help improve the mental function of everyone, no matter what age they are.

In another study that was done on animals, it was suggested that you can stimulate the brain in order to stop the nerve cells from shrinking, and this could even help to increase the size of the brain in some cases. Studies showed that rats that lived in enriched environments, or ones that have lots of challenges and toys, are going to have a larger outer brain along with healthier and bigger brain cells. And those that were given a lot of mental exercises tended to have more dendrites, which are the part of the brain that makes it easier for the cells to communicate back and forth with each other.

How does this correlate back to humans? Research has also been done on memory for humans as they age. It has found that in later years, having an environment that is stimulating and maybe brings in a few challenges on occasion, can help to grow those dendrites so the brain is able to communicate between the different cells. But if the environment around the person, no matter their age, becomes dull and boring, then this can impede the growth of these dendrites.

The important thing to remember here is that as you age, you may not be able to learn or remember things quite as quickly as you did in the past, such as when you were in school, but you will be able to learn and remember things just as well, if not better, then you did before. Often the issues that come with aging and your memory have nothing to do with simply aging, it is more likely caused because the brain is not used on a regular basis. No matter what age you are, make sure that you stimulate your brain and keep it active. If you can do this, memory loss is not going to be an issue that you have to deal with.

Chapter 2

WHAT CAUSES MEMORY PROBLEMS

Memory problems are something that everyone deals with on occasion. People will often end up worrying about misplacing things, or not being able to remember a certain important date that they should. This is pretty common and is going to happen to everyone at some point or another.

In this chapter, we are going to take a look at some of the main memory problems that you may face, some of the possible causes of these memory problems, and more.

Possible Causes of Memory Problems

A bit of memory loss is common in most of us. Maybe we were distracted when we met someone new, and then we couldn't remember their name later on. New mothers often forget things as they try to adjust to the new sleeping schedule with a baby. Maybe we are tired or stressed out from work causing it to become hard to handle the memories and remember the things that we should. There are a lot of different causes for memory loss. But the good news is that most of us are able to fix some of these issues with a few minor adjustments. Let's take a look at some of the most common reasons that you may be dealing with memory loss.

First, medication can sometimes cause a bit of memory loss. There are several over the counter and prescription medications that will interfere with our memory, and even cause memory loss. Some of the most common culprits of this include pain medications for surgery, sleeping pills, muscle relaxants, anti-anxiety medications, antihistamines, and antidepressants.

Drugs, tobacco and alcohol usage, can all cause some issues with your memory if you use them in excess. Excessive alcohol consumption on a regular basis has long been seen as a major cause of memory loss. In addition, smoking can harm your mind and memory because it will reduce the amount of oxygen that the brain gets. Studies have shown that those who smoke will often have more trouble putting a name to the face compared to those who don't smoke. In addition, illicit drugs can be dangerous to your memory because they will change up the way the chemicals react in the brain, making it much harder to recall memories.

If you are low on sleep, then your memories may be affected. The quality and the quantity of sleep are very important when it comes to memory. Not getting enough sleep on a regular basis, or if you wake up often during the night, this can lead to fatigue, which will really interfere with your brain's ability to consolidate and retrieve information when it's needed later on.

Stress and depression are some more causes to memory loss. When you have feelings of depression, it is hard for you to focus and pay attention to anything, which is going to affect the memory. In addition, anxiety and stress can also get in the way of how much you are able to concentrate. When you are tense, or your mind feels distracted and overstimulated, the ability to remember things will suffer. Also stress that is caused by some kind of emotional trauma can lead to memory loss as well.

There are some studies that suggest having a nutritional deficiency in certain nutrients can cause you to have some issues with your memory. For example, if your diet is low in high quality fats and proteins, it can be a cause to impairing your memory. In addition, being low on vitamin B12 and B1 can specifically cause some issues with your memory.

If you have been in an accident or another situation where you have suffered a head injury, then this could be a cause of memory impairment and damage that could affect you greatly. Any kind of severe hit to your head, such as from an accident, has been shown a lot of the time to cause some sort of injury leading to long term and short term memory loss. Depending on the situation and the severity of the injury, the memory may be able to improve over time.

It is also possible to suffer from memory loss from dementia, and this can lead to diseases like Alzheimer's. These are much more serious issues to deal with, and most of the time, the memory loss that you are dealing with is not going to be that bad. If you are dealing with dementia or any of the diseases associated with it, it is important to talk with your doctor right away to see what you are able to do. Since most memory issues are not going to be this bad, which allows you to improve them over time.

Identifying Memory Problems at Home, Work, and in Relationships

All of us will be forgetful at times. Just when we think we can remember the name of someone, it often will escape us. We try to remember things like where we put that important paperwork or our car keys, and yet we still can't find them. Forgetting things on occasion is not really a sign of a memory problem. Often it is just a sign that we weren't focusing enough on the issue at hand, and so the mind wasn't able to properly encode it at that time.

However, there are times when you may be dealing with memory problems, and it is important to learn the best ways to deal with these issues. Without working on the right techniques and with the right tools from the beginning, it is possible that the memory issues will become worse.

Now, there are some early memory issues that you may deal with. These are usually not too severe, and if you just experience one or two on occasion, there isn't much to be concerned about. But when the issues start to happen more frequently, or you experience quite a few of them, it is time to make changes to ensure your memory loss gets better, rather than worse. Some of the early signs that you should watch out for when it comes to memory problems include:

- ❖ Your personality may change. Maybe you start to get angry for no reason and your behavior all of a sudden becomes inappropriate.
- ❖ You commonly misplace items and can't ever seem to find them.
- ❖ You start to have trouble with the words you use. It's more than a slip of the tongue and can make communication difficult with others.
- ❖ You start to get lost or confused if you go off course, and sometimes even on routes that you are familiar with.
- ❖ It often becomes more difficult for you to make decisions.
- ❖ You run into more difficulty with any task that requires you to put in some thought. This could include something as simple as balancing your check book.
- ❖ Difficulty doing well at work. This can be due to the fact that you have more issues getting along with people, or because you can't

remember the details of a particular project and often start to make more mistakes.
❖ Forgetting important dates or double booking yourself on certain dates because you've forgotten about prior engagements.

These memory problems can easily start to creep into your life and can make things more difficult. When it comes to your home life, things can become difficult because you are always loosing things, forgetting how to complete certain tasks, and even getting lost on routes that are familiar to you. This will usually give you the feeling of being trapped in your own home, and maybe can cause you to become anxious because you are constantly wondering what you are forgetting about.

Memory problems can cause issues with your work life as well. Since you are worried about forgetting things, and worried that people will start noticing that you forget things, you may feel tenser and have trouble getting along with others. You may start to forget important details about a project or something else that you are working on, causing friction as others will have to pick up the work.

It is even possible to run into some issues with your personal life or your relationships. Often relationships will be affected by things like not being able to remember certain dates or important events that are going on in your partners life, and also other that involve money and paying bills.

Memory problems can affect almost every part of your life. It may seem like such a simple thing, and you may not feel that forgetting a thing here or there is a big deal, but as things progress, it can start to affect every part of your life. The good news is that you can work on these things. Just because you are already forgetting a few things here and there doesn't mean that you are doomed to just see more and more memory loss. If you work on strengthening your mind and working on your memory, you will be able to improve the different aspects of your life as well.

Are You Burnt Out Mentally? What Are the Signs?

Mental burnout is sometimes a common occurrence when your brain is overactive. Feelings of being overwhelmed by all of the responsibilities and tasks that you have to handle on a daily basis can make you feel lots of frustration and mental unrest. You will often have emotions of envy of others who seem to be more laid back and relaxed than you are, and your levels of mental stress can make things worse.

When you spend a ton of mental effort on any task, this will usually lead you to become mentally exhausted. While this does happen occasionally even for those who are otherwise healthy, it can be manageable in the beginning, but over time, it can cause a lot of issues, especially when it comes to maintaining your focus. This can leave you with low concentration levels and leads to more mistakes in your work than normal. You can even start to feel things like depression, irritation, and stress which just leads you to a downward spiral, and can affect your overall health in no time.

Mental exhaustion is often recognized when the individual feels burnt out from excess and long-term stress. While this is something that we all experience at least a little bit on occasion, the symptoms can become worse over time if you don't pay attention and work on it. If mental exhaustion carries on for too long, it can manifest itself into other symptoms such as behavioral, emotional, and physical. Some of the different side effects that you could experience when dealing with mental burnout include:

1. Physical symptoms: There are a number of physical symptoms that you may experience if the burnout is going on for too long. You may feel like you are exhausted and tired the majority of the time. You may have a higher tendency of feeling sick, lots of headaches, muscle aches, and back pain. Some people that endure mental exhaustion for a long period will sometimes see some changes in their sleep habits and appetite.

2. Emotional symptoms: If the emotional symptoms show up, you may have feelings of being helpless or like you are trapped and defeated by all of the mental stress you are under. The sense of self-doubt and failure can take over a lot of your thoughts at all parts of the day, which means that you are more likely to isolate yourself and then develop a more pessimistic view of the world, and of your life, in general.

3. Behavioral symptoms: It is common for those with mental exhaustion to spend less time with

their family and friends because they are just too tired and worn out to make the effort. If you notice that you are procrastinating more often and you are withdrawing from some of your other responsibilities, this can be a sign as well. You may notice that some of your eating habits change, sometimes you'll eat more, and sometimes you'll eat less. Depending on the individual and the severity of the mental exhaustion, the use of drugs or alcohol to cope with the extra stress is a sign that you need to watch out for as well.

For the most part, mental exhaustion is not something that is going to occur in a big fell swoop and all at once. It usually is going to accumulate over time. Being overworked, having too much to handle during the day, or just having too many things going on in your life can cause you to reach a boiling point, or the point where the body and the mind just aren't able to cope anymore. When this happens, you will start to see the symptoms show up.

All of us think that we are invincible and can handle as much stress as we want. But at some point, the stress is going to be too much. When we reach our capacity for dealing with stress, it can push us into a state of mental fatigue. In some cases, this brings about many health issues including chronic illness, autoimmune disorders, heart disease, and depression.

The good news is that there are ways that you can recover from mental exhaustion. It is amazing how resilient the body and mind can be, and are able to repair themselves from the injuries and symptoms that come from mental exhaustion. The biggest challenge here is that you must admit that you need to make a change. This helps you to not feel so guilty about making the change and helps you recharge your energy. Some of the other things that you can do to help yourself and your mind recover from mental exhaustion include:

1. Find some time to relax: Often stress is going to accumulate and take over because we don't take time for ourselves and time to relax. If there isn't an outlet to relieve stress in your life, it will just stay around and just compound, causing a bunch of stress related symptoms. Finding even a few minutes a day to collect

your thoughts and relieve stress can help you out so much. Taking a bath, reading a book, going on a walk, or just sitting quietly on your own can all help with this.

2. Reduce any sensory stimulation: Being around a lot of extra light and noise can really bombard the senses, which will lead to more stress. Your body is going to feel its most relaxed when you sit down in a dimly lit and quiet room, with as few distractions as possible. All of the constant sensory stimulation that comes from our phones and our screens can cause eye fatigue, headaches, and insomnia. If you need a sensory reset, consider going camping or visiting a park for a bit to help out.

3. Learn how to prioritize: Not all things are going to be worth your time to do. Sometimes the things that are the most unimportant are going to be the biggest contributors to your levels of stress. Recognizing the things that are actually important, and then letting go of the rest can help alleviate some of the mental exhaustion that you may be feeling.

Remembering Names and Faces

There are a lot of different ways that our mind can start to cause us problems and our memory can start to fail us. But many times people will have trouble with either faces, names, and numbers. Whether you deal with memory issues on all three of these, or just on one or two, it can be frustrating and can even cause problems in your personal and professional life. If you have some trouble remembering these things, you're not alone. There are many people who struggle with this issue, and often it is because the brain is wired to remember faces better than names. Often the best thing that you can do to help with this problem is to pay attention, and to use some different tricks to ensure the memory can do its job.

The first thing that you need to do is pay attention to the name. One of the best ways to learn the name of a person is to pay attention and really use your concentration when you hear the name for the first time. You can repeat the name a few times in your head to help it sit in your memory. Any time that you are in a situation where you meet someone, you may find that you get caught up in the moment, and you won't pay as much attention to their name as you probably should. During this time, you want to make sure that the name is actually able to enter your mind, rather than having it go in one ear and out the other.

If you find that you got caught up in the situation and you don't remember that person's name, even while in the same situation and conversation, then make sure to ask for it again. Most people won't mind telling it to you again, and this is another way to ensure that you can remember the name later on.

Another thing that you can do is after someone introduces themselves to you, stop and repeat their name right away. It doesn't have to be awkward, simply saying something like "Hello, Abby, nice to meet you" can help you to say the name again without making things sound strange. Being able to repeat the name out loud can solidify it in your brain because now you have said it and heard it. You may also want to say the name again, one or two times, to help you solidify this a bit more.

Making associations with the name can work to your advantage as well. Sometimes you will have a better time remembering the name if you try to make an alliterative association back to the name. For example, if you meet someone named Joe and he tells you he is from Jonesville, you could say something, in your own head, like "Joe joins us from Jonesville. The repetition of J can help you to have a better time remembering the name.

You can also consider doing a bit of rhyming in the mix as well. If you are able to come up with something that rhymes with the name, it helps it stick in your in your memory. With the name of Joe that we used before, you could go with a rhyme of "Joe knows how to tow", especially if he owns a towing company. If nothing seems to come to mind, then you can use a visual cue and make something up that will help you remember a bit better.

There are some people who run into issues with numbers as well. Numbers, especially ones that are a bit longer, are always a challenge. Turning them into words can sometimes make a difference when you want to remember them. You could come up with your own system, such as 1 = A, 2 = B and so on. From there, you would just make up your own acronym for the letters you have, and that can help you remember even the longest of numbers.

Often we have to take a few extra steps to ensure that we remember names, faces, and numbers. They aren't just going to stick because we want them to. We may have to go through and add some meaning to them to help them make more sense to us.

How Focus, Concentration, and Observation Affect the Memory Process

Studies have found that the amount that you focus or concentrate on something, the easier it is to store that event or information in your memory. If you are having trouble remembering things, perhaps the main issue here isn't that your memory is lacking, but rather, it could be due to the fact that you aren't paying enough attention to the things that are going on around us.

There are several reasons why our focus may be out and why we may not be able to pay attention to the things that we should. The first issue is that our brains are wired to drown out a lot of the extra noise. There is just so much that goes on around us. If we actually tried to pay attention to it all, we would go insane pretty quickly. The mind has learned how to turn a lot of this off so that we can work on focusing on just what is important, rather than on all the other little things that aren't that important.

The problem comes when we stop focusing on anything. In our modern world, we are often so busy running from one thing to another, that our focus and concentration is on too many little things, rather than on the important things. This confuses the brain, and it may have trouble figuring out what it should pay attention to at all. The brain isn't suffering from memory problems—it is dealing with a lack of focus problem instead.

The mind is trained to block out a lot of things like certain noises, and events that go on around us. If our mind failed to do this, it would cause our lives to be somewhat of a struggle due to us always trying to take in a million things at once.

A good exercise that you can try out is to go out for a walk. During this walk, try to pay attention and focus on the things that are around you. Do you hear the birds chirping? Can you tell if there is more than one type that is making noise at the moment? Can you pay attention to the smells? Do you notice the smell of the freshly cut grass, the flowers, the air, and the sun? Can you feel the hard pavement under your feet, or perhaps you took your shoes off and can feel the softness instead?

Focusing your mind in this way, even for just a few minutes a day, can do some wonders when it comes to improving the memory that you have. This method allows you to retrain your brain, helping it to develop and teach it what to focus on and ultimately improving your memory as well.

Memory Recall

The recall or the retrieval of memory is going to refer back to the re-accessing of events or information from the past. These events and the information has already been encoded and stored in the brain at some point in the past. This is a process that we often refer to as remembering. During the process of recall, the brain is going to replay back for us a neural activity pattern, one that was generated originally in response to one event or another. This helps to echo back the perception the brain had about the event. This process is so similar to thinking that there isn't really much of a distinction between thinking and remembering.

Of course, the replays that you see are not going to be identical to what you saw with the original. If this were true, we would have trouble telling the difference and fall into an issue with mixed awareness as we wouldn't know the difference between the memory and the genuine experience. One way that the differences show up is that memories won't be frozen in time. There are new information and some suggestions that can become incorporated into some of your older memories as time goes on. This is why remembering is sometimes known as an act of creative reimagination.

Due to the manner in which memories are stored and encoded, you will find that memory recall can be a reconstruction of elements that have been stored in different parts of the brain. Despite what we have thought for years, memories aren't going to be stored like books in a library. They aren't even stored as a collection of video clips and pictures. Instead, they are like a collage where the various elements are stored in separate parts of the brain, and then they are linked back together through associations and neural networks.

When we want to recall a memory, there is going to be a need for revisiting the nerve pathways of the brain, the ones that were formed there when the brain encoded the memory in the first place. How strong these pathways are can determine how easy it is for us to recall that memory.

The efficiency that humans are able to recall their memories is pretty amazing. Many times the things that we work to remember will occur from direct retrieval, where items of information will be linked right to a cue or a question, rather than through a sequential scan like a computer is often going to use. Then there are memories that are going to be brought out with the help of hierarchical inference, where a specific question is going to be linked back to some information when you know certain facts. Sometimes, the brain has the power to decide ahead of time whether it is worth its time to search for a fact or a memory. For example, if someone asked you what Aristotle's telephone number is, the brain therefore would know that is silly and wouldn't work on trying to find the memory.

When it comes to memory recall, there are going to be two main methods that you can use including recall and recognition. First is recognition that is going to be an association of an event, or an object, with one previously encountered or experienced. This is going to involve some comparisons within the brain. This is often a process that we are unconscious about and the brain even has some areas that are solely dedicated to face recognition so that we can recognize others we have met before, without having to go through and search for the information.

Many times, recognition is going to be seen as a superior skill compared to recall mostly because it is a bit more effective. It only relies on one process instead of two. This is because the process of recognition is going to be a familiarity decision while a full recall is going to require a search and retrieval of the item from the memory. From there, the recall process will rely on the familiarity decision to ensure that you pick the right answer to form the choices.

It is possible to increase the efficiency of memory recall in some cases, simply by making some inferences from our personal stockpile of knowledge about the world, and by the use of schema in the process. To help here, a schema is going to be an organized mental structure of pre-conceived ideas about the world around us and how this world works. We can then use this information to make assumptions that are realistic and that helps us to interpret the world that is around us.

With that said, there are going to be three different types of recall that are important to know about. These include:

1. **Free recall:** This is the process where a person is given a list of the items they need to remember, and then they will be asked to recall those items in any order they want. This is going to be the recall you use to display evidence of either the primary effect, which is when the person is able to recall items presented at the beginning of the list earlier and more often, then it shows the recency effects as well, when the person is able to recall the items that were at the end of the list better. Sometimes the contiguity effect is going to occur though, which is a tendency of the individual for items

from neighbouring positions on the list to be recalled the most successfully.

2. **Cued recall:** This is a process where a person will be given a list of items that they need to remember. When they are tested, they will be given guides and cues to happen. When the cues are provided to these test subjects, they are more likely to remember the items on the list, even if they had trouble before. This can also be done with the stimulus response recall. This is when numbers, pictures, and words are shown on a page together to help you remember things better.

3. **Serial recall:** This is the ability of some people to recall events or items in the order that those things occurred. This would include events that were chronological or autobiographical memories. It can even include things like the ordering of sentences to help them make sense. Serial recall that occurs in the long term memory is going to be different compared to those that show up in the short term memory. When serial recall has been tested, there are several general rules that are going to show up including:

a) Events that are more recent are the ones that are easier for people to remember.
b) The recall is going to decrease if the list or the sequence starts to increase.
c) There is going to be a tendency to remember the correct items, but the order is often going to be harder to get right.
d) When there are errors being made, there is sometimes a tendency of the individual to respond with an item that resembles the original item in some way. So, they may say dog instead of fog if they were given a list of words to remember.
e) Sometimes there are going to be errors in repetition, but these are often pretty rare.
f) If the person recalls an item on the list earlier than it was listed, then there is a tendency to insert the missed item right after.
g) If an item from a previous trial is recalled during the current trial, it is more likely to be recalled at the position it was at in the original trial.

Memory recall is a process that everyone goes through when they want to be able to remember or bring out a memory after the mind has already gone through and encoded that memory. Being able to do this recall can make it easier to bring out old memories and information at any time that we need. For those who have trouble with recalling items, there is often an issue with the encoding process, and that is the first thing they need to explore and try to fix.

Let's Test Your Memory

Now we are going to get started on a simple test that you are able to use in order to help test out your memory and how well it is doing. This is just a basic one to get you thinking about how well your memory is doing. You can go through and try out some other options later as you practice your memory and work to get better. There are many options online that you can use as well.

For the following questions, answer these with the following answers:

>Always- 1
>
>Often- 2

Sometimes- 3

Rarely- 4

Almost Never -5

Let's get started.

1. Do you find that it is often hard for you to remember phone numbers and the names of people you meet?
2. How often do you have to stop and try to remember where you placed everyday items? This can include options like your wallet, keys, glasses, and more.
3. How often do you have to go through and replace the passwords that you have, whether verbal or numerical, because you can't remember what the original one was?
4. How often do you stop and ask yourself "What was I about to do next"?
5. How often do you end up double-booking or scheduling yourself, because you forgot that you had previous plans in place with someone else?

6. How often do you need to ask someone near to you to repeat instructions or even a story that they were telling you simply because you weren't able to remember what they told you the first time?
7. How often do you have trouble when it comes to remembering where the car is parked?

For this test, the lower the score the worse your memory is at this time. This means that you almost always, or often, forget important and everyday things like where your keys are or the names of people you meet. The higher your score, the better your memory is. For this test you should have had a test score of somewhere in between 25-35. This would of shown you that your memory is ok and of average. Anything below might give you the indication that you need to try and focus on sharpening your memory skills up for the future

But before you start fretting and no matter what you scored in the test, there are things that you can do in order to improve your memory. All of us need help with our memory at some point, and this test just gives you a realistic idea of where you are starting so you can make the right changes.

We will take a look in the next chapter at some of the different techniques that you can use to help improve your memory. If you take a few tests, including the one above, and you are not happy with the results that you get, don't be upset with yourself. Using the different techniques that we discuss in this guidebook will help you to get your memory to a higher level, no matter where you were at the beginning of this journey.

Chapter 3

Memory Improvement Techniques and Exercises

Now that we have spent some time talking about human memory and how it works, it is time to look at some of the ways that you can improve your memory as well. Seeing improvement when it comes to our memory's ability to remember things, is something that we would all like. Remembering things such as names, faces, and facts, with ease is something that would make life so much easier. With the techniques that are presented next, you will be able to gradually improve your memory as time goes on.

Stop Multitasking

Multitasking is something that we are taught to do at a young age and is something that we are pretty used to working with. We often think that it is the best way to get as much done as possible in a short amount of time. With how busy we are in our daily lives, we figure that the only way to keep going and not fall behind, is to simply just multitask.

There are many studies out there that talk about how bad multitasking can be for you. It may seem like a great idea, and one of the things that you need to do to stay on top of things, but this is simply not true. Not only is it really slowing down the work that you need to complete compared to doing each task on its own, but it is also making it hard on your memory to remember what you need.

Multitasking is the shorthand for individuals to try and do as many things at the same time as possible. In the long run, the process of multitasking can actually slow you down, can make you very forgetful, and even makes you more prone to errors as you go along.

In fact, research has shown that you need at least eight seconds to memorize most things. So, if you are talking on the phone to someone, carrying in the groceries, and put your car keys down whilst doing these things, it isn't very likely that you will remember where you have put them.

It is much better for your memory to avoid doing multitasking as much as possible. Instead of working with multitasking, you should consider working with mindfulness. Mindfulness is going to help you to achieve a focus that is undistracted. For example, students who decided to take a class on mindfulness found that they were able to score better on reading comprehension as well as their capacity for working memory. These students also found that they had fewer thoughts that distracted them from the task at hand.

If you end up in a situation where you are trying to work on five tasks (or more at the same time, it is a good idea to stop yourself. Instead of focusing on all five, make sure that you focus your attention on the task at hand. If you notice that a thought that is distracting starts to enter your head, remember that these aren't really reality, and try to not think about them by just focusing on the thing you were doing. You may even want to consider ending the day with a short meditation session so that you can work on stopping the wandering of your mind which will also help you to relax, and ensures that you get a more restful sleep at night.

Focus Your Attention

You will find that one of the major components to your memory and remembering various things is attention and what you focus that attention on. To ensure that the information you want to hold onto is able to move over from the short term to the long term memory, then you must attend to this information. There is just too much going on around you for the brain to focus on everything. Often this means that the mind will have to pick and choose what information it wants to hold onto, and which information you will ignore.

Sometimes this means that you need to override the mind and choose what needs your attention. You can decide what is important and then focus all of your attention onto it, alerting the mind that this is something you want to remember in the future. One of the best ways that you can focus your attention is to make sure that you learn the information without a lot of distractions. Some of these distractions are easy to avoid, such as turning off the music, turning off the television, and ensuring that your computer and your phone won't cause a distraction to you. Other times, avoiding distractions, such as noisy children or your roommate, can be quite hard. You may need to find some time to be alone to do memorization or find another place to be during that time.

Avoid Cramming

This is something that you can use if you need to get ready for a big test at school, but it can also be helpful if you have a big presentation that you need to give at work. In fact, it works no matter what situation you end up in where you must remember a lot of information in order to prepare for that specific situation at hand.

Cramming is one of the worst things that you can do. Remember that the memory is only able to hold onto about seven items at one time. You can do chunking and organization and other options in order to help hold onto new information as well. Mnemonic devices are something that can help you hold onto more information also. But there is a limit to how much the brain is able to hold onto during a specific period of time. The brain has its limits and by cramming too much information into it, especially at one time, it will usually hit a limit and struggle to take in any more.

It is much better to study material over several sessions, with these sessions spaced out far enough apart. This allows you to keep filling up the brain, without overdoing the amount that it is able to handle. Research has shown over and over again that students who study on a regular basis, for shorter sessions are able to remember the material a lot better, often leading them to do better on tests than other who don't.

Be Organized and Structured

When you are surrounded by chaos, it is hard to concentrate on tasks, and things you are trying to do. Disorganization and clutter are often things that will distract you, due to drawing you from what you were doing, to wanting to clean up the mess and tidy up. This will often lead to things that are really your priority to get done, getting postponed as a result of this.

Researchers have found that information organized inside of the memory in clusters are related. You are able to use this information to your advantage if you structure and organize all of the material that you are trying to study. For example, you may find that it is useful to group together concepts and terms that are similar. Or you may want to make a good outline of your readings and notes so that you can go back through and group together the concepts that are related.

Relate the Information Back to Things You Know

No matter what, there are already situations and people you know in your life. Whether they are something from your past or something that you are very familiar with now, you can use this to your advantage to help you improve your memory. This is really helpful if the material you are trying to learn is unfamiliar and you need some help with remembering it in your own life.

When you are working with material that is really unfamiliar to you, take some time to think about how that particular set of information can already relate to information that you know. When you are able to establish a good relationship between the ideas that are new and the previously existing memories, this will help you ensure that you are going to recall the information a lot easier.

Read the Information Out Loud

The more times that you are able to rehearse the information, the easier it is for you to remember. When you are trying to learn something new, especially if it is something that is difficult to remember, you may find that reading it out loud will help it sink in better. This may be due to the fact that not only are you reading the words on the page, but you are hearing them as well when your voice goes over them.

Research suggests that reading new information, or other reading materials, out loud, can significantly improve how well you are able to remember the material. Both psychologists and educators have found that when students have to learn new material, they are able to understand the information and recall it later better than before, after doing this. It has proven to leave a secondary blueprint of the information for the memory to store.

Trying Meditation

Meditation is a technique that can help you to calm down your mind and reduce stress that you may have built up. It may not directly work on the memory like some of the other techniques, but since it works on things like clearing the mind, introducing mindfulness, reducing stress, and leaving you overall feeling more relaxed, it can work wonders for helping you free up your mind, and make more room for you to remember things, in the future.

There are a ton of benefits that come with meditation. Just by reducing the amount of stress that you feel on a regular basis, and helping you learn how to slow down and relax, meditation can prevent many health conditions that may be plaguing you. There are a lot of different methods of meditation that you can choose to work with, which makes it easier to find one that you like and suits you.

You can do meditation on your own, or if you'd prefer you can always choose to go with guided meditation instead. Most of the time the meditation session should be in a quiet environment with no sound, but you may use some soft music or utilize a word or mantra to help you have something to focus on.

If you want to utilize meditation to help with your memory, there are a few different methods that you can try. We are going to take some time to look at one of the basic meditation sessions that you can do. It is very simple and it can last as long as you want it to, but going for at least five to ten minutes is usually ideal to help you relax and get the full benefits.

To start with, make sure that you are able to sit in a place that is quiet and where you can be left alone for at least ten to fifteen minutes. You will want to sit down on the floor and get comfortable. Have your legs crossed, your back stacked nice and straight so that the air from breathing can easily fill up your lungs. Leave your hands on your lap. If sitting on the floor is not comfortable for you, it is fine to either put a cushion underneath you to keep your alignment right, or you can sit in a chair if you want, as long as your back stays straight and your feet are on the floor.

When you are ready to start, take in some deep and cleansing breaths and then close your eyes. Try to keep your mind clear, and just focus on the deep breaths that you are taking in and out. As a beginner, this can be fairly hard at first. Your mind will try to drift on to the things that have been happening and going on in your life, such as work, family life, and events. But try your best to keep all the memories and thoughts out of the way and keep your mind as clear as possible.

If thoughts start to creep into your meditation, try not to get mad or down about yourself. This will just make it harder. When those thoughts get into your mind, you will just need to gently push them aside to help clear your brain from this kind of thinking. This can take some practice, but the more that you work on the meditation process, the easier it is for you to accomplish this goal.

When the ten to fifteen minutes are done, you can take a few more deep breaths, and then slowly open your eyes. You can then get up and move on with the rest of your day. It is best if you can do at least one meditation session each day. It is up to you how long you would like it to last, whether you would like to do it in the morning or evening, whatever works well for you.

Live a Life That Is Blessed and Happy

The happier and healthier you are able to live your life, the better your memory is going to become. The lesser negativity you have in your life the more this will boost your memory and help you to recall more. There are several different things that you can do to help make this happen, and working to implement each one will do wonders when it comes to your memory and how well it works.

The first thing that you will want to do is make sure that you can get your life organized. A life that is disorganized and cluttered can bring about a lot of forgetfulness. You should spend some time organizing your home and your office. Everything that is there either needs to have its own personal place, if you have things that are not essential and needed, it would be ideal to remove these things. You can choose to use a day planner or your smartphone to take notes on tasks, appointments, and other events that are going to happen during the week so you stay as organized as possible.

You may also find that taking notes and writing down any information that is important, such as meetings, names, and discussions that you don't want to forget can help reinforce the power of learning and remembering, even down the line. In addition to writing down the information, consider repeating the information or the name out loud, at least once when you first hear it like we have talked about previously.

Socializing can be an important aspect of this as well. People who isolate themselves and only go out on occasion will often miss out on the socialization aspect that is needed. Spending time with others, conversing with them, and learning new things for these individuals can go a long way in helping you to keep the mind sharp. A rich and full social life can help to prevent depression and stress and keeping your social calendar as full as you can will help prevent a decline in memory.

Another thing that you can try when you are working to live a life that is blessed and happy is to laugh more. Unlike other emotions that you may experience, laughter is able to engage more than one region of the brain and research has shown that it can also be beneficial to your memory. The more time that you spend laughing during the day, the better your memory will be.

There are many ways that you can work to improve your memory through laughter. You may want to try to join a Laughter club and participate as much as possible. You may want to spend time with children enjoying their stories and fun ideas. You can surround yourself with people who are playful, fun-loving, and like to laugh as well. Maybe try putting up some funny pictures around your home that will at least make you smile when you see them. Try watching something that is funny like a comedy program or movie, in the morning or before bed to ensure that you get at least a little bit of laughter into your day, to help brighten up your mood.

Getting Enough Sleep

Harvard Research shows that people are 33 percent more likely to infer connections among ideas that are related distantly after they sleep. But what is really interesting is that few realize that their performance got better after they slept. Sleep can also help to make your memories more effective and can help you practice and improve your performance when it comes to some of your more challenging skills. In fact, it only takes one night of getting no more than six hours of sleep in order to impact how clearly you are able to think the next day.

We have all had this happen at some point, when we have to stay up late due to things like studying, socializing with friends or trying to get our kids to sleep, causing us to get a lack of sleep. The after effect of this will usually cause us to forget things easily and lead us to make a lot of mistakes as we stumble through the day. Often that day is much harder to get through compared to some of the others, and we can't wait to just get it over with so we can go back to sleep.

The process that is known as neuroplasticity, or brain growth, is believed to underlie the capacity and the ability of the brain to control behavior. This includes our memory and how we learn. Plasticity is going to occur when the neurons start to receive stimulation from the information, for events, or from the environment that is around us.

In addition, there are certain types of long-term potentiation, that can be elicited in sleep. The potentiation is going to be a neural process that is going to be associated with the laying down of memory and learning. This suggests that the connections between the synapsis are going to become stronger when you get to sleep. Not sleeping enough, will cause these connections to not form as well as before.

This is also something that applies to infants. Research shows that even small naps can be what the baby needs in order to boost their brainpower. In specific, infants who slept in between their learning and then their testing sessions, found that they had a better ability to recognize patterns in new information. This showed researchers that there is a big change in memory that can help with the cognitive development of the baby.

It is believed that this can be the same for many adults too. It is believed that taking a nap in the afternoon could help to restore and boost your brainpower. Plus, it can make things easier if you are lacking in sleep at night because of other things going on. What this means is that if you are looking to boost your cognitive power, going to bed early, or taking a nap in the afternoon, may be the best way to make this happen.

Playing Brain Games

Playing brain games is another way to stretch your mind allowing it to work harder than it has done before. If you don't spend some time to challenge your brain the proper way with surprising and new information, over time it is going to start to deteriorate. What the research about brain plasticity shows us is that when we provide the brain with the right kind of stimulus, then you will have the key to counteract the degermation that would normally happen.

There are a variety of methods that you can use in order to add in a challenge for the brain including methods such as using brain games. You can find these on a variety of websites, they will usually give you scores at the end so you know how well you have done. A good website like Lumosity.com is a great place to start.

Dr. Michael Merzenich, a professor emeritus at the University of California, is one of the pioneers of research into neuroplasticity and brain plasticity for over 30 years. He has been able to develop brain training programs for the computer that can help you to work on a large range of memory and mental skills such as improving memorization and reading comprehension. This is a program that is known as Brain HQ which has a ton of exercises that you can use to help you work on your memory, to increase your mental power, and even allows you to keep track of the progress that you are making over time.

Some people will like to spend their time doing things like word finds or Sudoku and crossword puzzles, to help build up their memory. These are things that can be done from anywhere and at any time, and are things that can help you out a lot.

If you do decide to implement brain games into your routine to improve your memory, then it is ideal if you invest a minimum of 20 minutes a day on this. Of course, make sure that you divide that up between a few different tasks, such as five to seven minutes per task, as spending too much time on one task is not beneficial.

According to Dr. Merzenich, whom we have mentioned previously, the primary benefits are going to show up in the first five minutes or so of doing the task. Any longer than this and you will risk getting bored or mental fatigue, therefore not letting you reap the benefits.

Of course, you should only really be doing brain games if you find that they actually stimulate and interest you. For some people, these tasks are just going to be another thing that they need to be able to fit into their schedule. They may find them boring and no fun at all. If this sounds like you, don't try to force yourself into doing them. You need to focus on things that are interesting and stimulating for yourself. If the brain games don't do it for you, consider working on a new skill or hobby, or find another option to help you out.

Master a New Skill

One thing that you may want to try out when you are working on improving your memory is including mastering a new skill. Your mind is always looking for something new to learn, as it gets tired of learning the same thing over and over again. Over time, you will find that the memory just kind of stagnates, rather than grows, which can cause you to lose memory instead of improving it.

Engaging in a meaningful and purposeful activity, it is going to do wonders when it comes to stimulating your neurological system. Doing this can also help things such as, countering the effects of any diseases related to stress, reducing your risk of developing dementia, and enhancing your wellbeing and health. Just simply working on mastering a new skill, will allow you to challenge your mind in the way it needs.

A key factor in helping you improve the functioning of your brain, or even reversing some of the functional declines is the seriousness of purpose with which you engage in a new task. What this means is that you can't just go sit there mindlessly in a class on a new subject, without feeling any care or passion about that topic. The task needs to be something that is important and somehow interesting and meaningful to you. Something that will actually challenge you and get your attention.

One study found that doing various craft activities, such as knitting and quilting, were associated with a decreased likelihood of having mild cognitive impairment. This is good news for those who want to make sure that your mind stays sharp, even as you age.

There is another study that was published that found that spending at least a little of your time doing an activity that was cognitively demanding, such as digital photography, learning a new language, or even learning how to quilt, can help to enhance the functioning of the memory. Any activity can work as long as it keeps the mind active and will hold your interest for an extended period of time.

The key here is to find some kind of activity that is stimulating for your brain. This means that it must be an activity that will require your undivided attention while also giving you some satisfaction for doing the work. It also needs to be some kind of activity that you are excited about and are going to look forward to doing. You can choose the activity that you want to go with, as long as you pick one that is going to challenge your mind in some way that you are not used to. Some of the different activities that you can try out include things like crafting, building, gardening, language learning, or playing an instrument.

Trying Mnemonic Devices

Another option that you can work with is a mnemonic device. These are techniques that you are able to use to help you improve how well you remember something. It is basically a memory technique that you can use to help your brain encode and recall information. It is just a simple shortcut that can help you to associate the information that you need to remember with a word, sentence, or an image depending on what works the best for you.

Mnemonic devices have been around for a long time and some of them can be dated back to the time of ancient Greece. Almost everybody already uses them, usually without even realizing. It is a simple way for you to help memorize information so that you can recall it later on when you need it a lot easier.

There are actually quite a few different types of mnemonic devices that you can choose to use. Each of them can be effective, but it will depend on your overall goals and what you are hoping to get with memorizing the information. Some of the most popular mnemonic devices that you can choose to use to help your memory includes:

The Method of Loci

This is a mnemonic device that originated from back in ancient Greek times, and is one of the oldest methods of memorizing that we know how to use today. This method is an easy one to work with. To do this, imagine in your head a place that you are pretty familiar with already. You can use something as simple as your home. The rooms in your house will become the objects of information that you need to memorize. Or you can choose to use the route that you usually take to get to school and work. Then you can use things to memorize along the way such as the landmarks.

With this method, you are going to go through a list of concepts and words that you need to memorize and then try to associate every word with one of the locations. You need to make sure that you have this in some type of order, so that you can retrieve all of the information that you need in the future.

Acronyms

Another skill that you can work with when it comes to mnemonic devices is an acronym. This is going to be a word that is formed with the first letters, or groups of letters, that show up in a phrase or a name. You can also work with an acrostic, which is a series of lines from which a particular letters form into a phrase or a word. This could include the first letters that come from all of the lines. You can use these as a type of mnemonic device by taking the first letters of words, or you can pick names that you need to remember and then develop your own acrostic or acronym.

Let's look at an example of this. In music, many students are going to have to learn the order that the notes are there to make it easier to identify and play the right note when the music is read. The notes that show up on the treble staff are going to be EGBDF. And the acrostic that is often used with this is going to be Every Good Boy Does Fine. Then when we look at the bass staff, the notes are ACEG. This one is often going to be the acrostic of All Cows Eat Grass.

You can always choose to make your own acronym based on the information that you are trying to remember. Keep the words in the order that you need to remember them by. This helps you to make an acronym that makes sense for your needs and ensures that not only do you remember the words or the information that you need but that you remember it in the right order.

Rhymes

A rhyme is a saying that is going to have a similar terminal sound when it gets to the end of every line. They are the way that we used to learn things when we were younger, and they can still be used often as adults if we just learn how to work with them the right way.

Rhymes are often seen as easier to remember because you not only get to remember the words, but they can be stored by acoustic encoding in your brain. Some examples of the rhymes that you may want to work with include:

In fourteen hundred and ninety-two, Columbus sailed the Ocean Blue.

Thirty days hath September

April, June, and November

All the rest have thirty-one

Save February, with twenty-eight days' clear

And twenty-nine each leap year.

If you have a lot of information that you have to remember for something, then a nice rhyme can always be helpful. You have to be pretty creative to make this happen, and you may need to look at some examples online or ask others to help you find the rhyming words that you need to make this work.

Organization and Chunking

The next option that you can work with is known as chunking. This is an easy way for you to break down some big pieces of information into smaller and more organized chunks so that you can manage the information easier than before. A good example of this technique is how telephone numbers in the United States are listed. There are ten digits for each number, and then they are broken down into three chunks. This makes it much easier to remember the phone number, rather than hoping that you can remember ten random numbers.

For most people, the short term memory is going to have some limitations, and this is usually about seven items of information. Because of this, being able to place the larger quantities of information into the smaller chunks or the smaller containers, will make it easier for the brain to hold onto.

You will find that organizing the information that you have into either subjective or objective categories can help out quite a bit. When you use objective organization, you are basically placing the information into well-recognized and logical categories. For example, grass and trees would go into plants, and crickets would be an insect.

You can also choose to work with what is known as a subjective organization. This is when you make categories of items that don't seem related, but you do it in a way that makes it easier to recall the information later. This is a useful skill to work with because it will take the information that you need to learn and then enable you to break it down. If you are able to divide a list of items into a few categories, then all you need to remember is the categories in order to remember the rest of the information.

Imagery

The last type of mnemonic device that we are going to explore is that of imagery. Visual imagery is going to be a great way for a lot of people to memorize different types of items. For example, you may use it in order to help you to memorize a pair of words, such as green grass, yellow sun, and blue water. If you are using the Method of Loci that we talked about before, it is possible that you are using some kind of imagery to help with memorization. When you are able to recall specific imagery, it is going to help you out quite a bit if you are able to recall information that is associated with some kind of imagery.

This method can work best when you want to remember smaller pieces of information. When you are trying to remember the name of someone you just met for example, you may want to try and use imagery. You might meet someone with the name of Peggy and then imagine a pirate with a wooden leg. Or maybe if you met someone named Harry, you may imagine a big grizzly bear. You can choose the imagery that you want to use for each item that you need to remember. But since the brain and the mind work well with images and pictures, it is one of the best methods to help you get the most out of your memory.

As you can see, there are many different options that you can choose to use in order to improve the brain and ensure that you are able to remember anything that you want, whether it is big or small. By trying out a few of these different techniques to determine which ones work and don't work for you.

The 4 Details Exercise

This is a good one to work with when you meet someone new, and you want to make sure that you are able to remember them. For this, when you encounter someone new, try to memorize a minimum of four details about that person. It doesn't have to be anything too complex. Maybe you remember that they wore black shoes, a big hat, had red hair and wore a pink coat. The goal here is to observe some details about that person, so that you can recall those details easier later in order to help you remember.

There are some scientists who see this as more of a passive memory technique. The reason being is that you are not relying on just a special technique. Instead, your just asking the brain to do the work for you. The reason that this is so important is that we often don't ask the mind to practice being observant enough. Because of this, we often fail to observe what is going on around us. We may also fail to observe the things that we don't see, such as making a visual image of any movement that we may be able to hear in other rooms that are near us.

If you are looking to be a better observer of the things that are occurring around you, then this is the best exercise that would help you. This is also something that you can scale. Maybe you will start with an observation of just one new person for the day. After time and when you become more experienced, you can then add in more information, more people, or a combination of both depending on what you are the most comfortable with.

Number Brain Exercises

One thing that a lot of people struggle with when they are working on their memories is remembering numbers that they need. Numeracy is a skill that is really important, and it is something that you definitely need to work on each day when your trying to strengthen your memory. One technique that you can use is the add 3, minus 7 exercise technique. It's pretty simple to use, and will get the brain working when it comes to numbers, so it is definitely something that is worth trying out.

To get yourself started with this technique, just pick out any three-digit number. Then you will add three to the digit, doing that three times. Then you will take that new number and minus seven from it, seven times. This means remembering all of the numbers you have chosen.

Keeping the numbers in order can be quite a challenge for your brain, but this will help in improving it, and when it comes to remembering things in the future.

You should try to do this exercise at least five times when you're trying it out for the first time. You can also add more digits, such as moving up to a four-digit number instead. If you want, you can also change up the numbers that you want to use, such as adding 12, 12 times and then minus 11, 11 times based on how much you want to progress and modify this exercise.

Doing Recall in Your Mind

While it is often best to say things out loud to help you remember them, there are some situations where this isn't ideal. Instead try to do the recall in your mind so that you can still say it, without looking silly in front of others.

You can simply follow any of the words that the other person is speaking by repeating those words in your own mind.

Now, imagine that you are in a conversation with someone, and they are telling you how they want to go to the movies tomorrow and see a new movie that has just come out. All you would need to do is repeat all of the words that the person uses to tell you about the movie, but repeat them in your head. This exercise works because you are asking your memory to recall information as it is happening. Of course, the more challenging the information that you ask the brain to keep up with, the more that you end up exercising the brain at the same time.

The Metronome Clapping Exercise

This is another great option that you can choose to work with. Try working with a Metronome if you happen to have one, or something similar, that can be just as ideal. But there are also videos online or other tools that you can use that work just as well. You can then set the metronome, or a similar sound, at a certain speed to then practice a technique that is known as covering the click.

While this one may not be as effective as some of the others when it comes to memory, it is going to work for improving your focus and your concentration. Both presence and concentration are going to be skills that we need to improve in order to help with the memory.

If you want to get better with this exercise, you may want to gradually increase the speed that the clicks happen. If you are able to start accurately covering the metronome with a long distance between the clicks, try speeding up the metronome in order to keep benefiting from this exercise.

Create Your Own Memory Palace

This is considered one of the best brain exercises that you can use, and is considered one of the easiest as well. All that it involves is making a simple drawing (you will make your own that no one is going to see, so don't worry about this). Of course, this simple drawing is going to have some principles that you need to follow in order to make this exercise work well.

So, why is a memory palace a powerful and effective exercise? First, the memory palace is going to work with some of your spatial memory. It can also be a good way to work on your autobiographical and recovered memory. When it comes to brain exercises, you will find that the memory palace is going to work in reverse to some of the other options that you work with. The reason for this is because you will access the cues that are already blueprinted on the mind, but may still be outside of your awareness.

While you may not be able to go into a brand new place or home and remember a ton of details, as if you were asked to remember the details of your own home or that of a friends. Creating a memory palace allows you to exercise the inborn ability that all humans have to remember certain details. Some people even use this idea to help when they are trying to remember or memorize something, such as trying to memorize all of the Prime Ministers of Canada.

Learn a New Language

This one is similar to learning a new skill or finding a hobby to keep you challenged, but you will find that learning a new language will be a great way to keep the mind sharp and working to its full potential. Bilingualism is perfect for the brain, and has been shown to improve cognitive skills, and also make you smarter.

Has there ever been a language that you might have been a little curious to learn? But never really had the time to do so? The good news about learning a foreign language is not only is it fun, but it can also help with your memory improvement. The main reason for this is that when you are learning a new language, you are continually asking the brain to bring out and recall information that you have previously learned.

You will find that learning a language is a great exercise for the brain not only because it provides a good challenge, but it gets you out there and talking and socializing with people. Regular conversation, especially in a new language, can be something that really stimulates the brain. You can increase the benefits of this further by even learning to sing in the new language. Singing has been shown to help increase cortisol and other chemicals that are needed for healing throughout the body. Because of this, learning a foreign language and singing it, at least sometimes, can help you increase the impact as well as the effectiveness of this kind of brain activity.

Working with a Mind Map

Mind mapping is usually a process that is done to help you make decisions and determine the best solution to get the results that you want. But you can utilize it in other aspects of your life to ensure that you keep the brain working as it should. Basically, you will start out with the problem that you want to fix, and then outline some of the various solutions that you think may work for it. You will keep going, following each course of action until you reach the one that makes the most sense.

The reason that the mind map works is that it forces you to stop and think about something critically. You aren't going to be limited by your emotions, and there will be a logical outcome that is based on facts and nothing else. You have to use this as a way to think in a more critical manner, learn how to come to a conclusion without any biases or emotions getting in the way. It is definitely a great way to think through some of the important decisions you often need to make.

Playing a Sport

As silly as it may seem, you will often find that playing a sport, especially a team sport where socialization is involved, can be a good way to improve your memory. But any type of sports activity in general such as things like working out at the gym with a partner can be highly beneficial also.

If you are doing something like just going to the gym and working out, you can make the brain work by memorizing the number of reps and sets that you need to do each time you train. You can also work on rehearsing the content of a program when you are on the treadmill. Or you can do the four detail exercise that we talked about before while observing some of the other people you encounter at the gym.

Working out at the gym can be a win-win. You get a chance to work out the body, meet new people, as well as using techniques to help improve your brain and memory at the same time.

As you can see, there are a ton of different techniques and brain exercises that you can choose to work with. Whether you are trying to use them in order to solve some of the real world problems that you are facing, or you are just trying to work with them in order to improve your memory, all of them can be used successfully. But this brings up the issues of which brain technique or exercise is the best one for you to use.

It is often going to depend on what issue of the memory you are trying to work on. Most of us have just one or two aspects that we will need to look into in order to improve. It is unlikely that we need to work on all aspects of the memory. Figuring out which areas of your thinking and your memory need the most improvement can help you to pick out the right exercises to do.

Since you are only supposed to spend about five minutes on each task, and for around 20 to 25 minutes a day on exercises, it is best to have at least a handful of techniques and exercises to help you out. You can set up a routine that you can follow on a daily basis, and then try to mix and match the exercises that will solve your particular memory problem, or the ones that work the best for your needs. There isn't really one particular memory exercise or technique that will work the best in every situation. You have to go through them all and pick the option that works the best for your needs and your own personal memory goals and then get started from there.

Chapter 4
Memory Improving in Your Day to Day Life

There are a lot of different things that you need to be able to remember during your day. These often include things like having to get the kids to school on time, remembering where you've put your keys, and important dates and appointments. But these can be basic things as compared to when you get to work and you have remember more complex things.

In addition to some of the techniques that we talked about above, there are a few daily routines that you can implement to help you improve your memory even more. These things can be as simple as starting an exercise routine, eating the right foods, playing memory games to keep the brain sharp, and socializing with those around you. Let's take a look at some of the basic things that you can do in your daily life to help you improve your memory in no time at all.

Exercising

The first thing that you can work on in order to improve your memory is exercising more regular. Exercising is one of the best things you can do for your whole body and your mind. Whatever type it maybe, exercise in general can be so beneficial when it comes to helping you in providing more oxygen and nutrients to your brain.

Many times as we age, we start to give up on exercising in our life. More than often we feel too tired and too weary to get up and get going. Other times we just may simply not have the time to do it. But other problems that may plague us like health issues, like pains and discomfort, weak bones, or balance problems. But there is always something out there you can do to suit you and your schedule.

Doing a wide range of exercises can be one of the best and beneficial ways to ensure that you are taking care of your mind as they all will play big factors towards improving it. Things like cardio and weight lifting has been shown to be good for the brain due to increasing the heart rate and getting more blood flow pumped to the brain.

Socializing

One thing to consider when you are working on your memory is that socializing can help. Being around others and talking with them can do wonders to ensuring your mind stays sharp and keeps working long into the future. A lot of the time we will be so busy with our own lives, we end up going long periods of time without talking to anyone else. This is a dangerous thing to get our-selves into because it can quickly lead to the decline of your mind.

This is another reason that some people may believe that their memories start to fade as they get older. As we age, we often find that our health and other factors force us to stay inside and maybe socialize less than we did in the past. But this is a bit of a dangerous thing to do. Socializing can help our brains stay sharp, but when we start to withdraw from society and from doing things that we enjoy, it is our mind and our memories that start to falter as a result.

Just doing the most basic of social activities will help you out a lot, such as going out for coffee with a close friend, joining a gym or doing some sort of evening classes. There is always something out there that will suit you, but always be willing try something new to help take your mind into new avenues, rather than keeping it to what it's already used to.

Mental Activities

A mind that is used on a regular basis is a strong mind, one that is able and willing to do anything that you ask of it. But a mind that sits there and just spends time on the computer or time watching television, is one that is going to waste away and will struggle with memory problems for many years to come. Regardless of your current mental activity level though, you can always add more of these activities into your routine to ensure that you make the mind as strong as possible.

Mental exercises can help to keep your brain working, and they don't have to be all that difficult. We have discussed previously of the many different exercises and things you can do such as puzzles, brain games and learning a new language.

While many people associate aging with the decline in their mental capacities, often the real issue lies more with their lack of working and exercising the brain. They will decide to sit at home and never try anything new or challenging. The mind needs to have a workout on occasion. It needs a chance to explore and learn new things. The more that you are able to do this, the less your memory is prone to fading over time.

Organizing Your Life

Sometimes the reason that we are not able to remember things is that our lives can be unorganized. The clutter around us can cause us to lose things, no matter how good our memory is. Taking some time to clear out the clutter and add some organization into your life could be the answer that you are looking for.

Clutter can cause us to become stuck thinking about mess, which can play a big role in our mental health. The messier a home is, the harder it is for our memories to work.

The best way to fix this problem is to learn how to cut down on the clutter as much as possible and implement some sort of organization into your life. The first step here is to go through the whole house, room by room if you have to, and start throwing things out. Many of us have a ton of stuff that just gets in the way and doesn't serve a purpose, or has lost its purpose that it once had.

This process can take some time, but once you declutter and get rid of many of the things that are just hanging around your home, taking up space and making it difficult for you to get things done in your daily life, you will be amazed at how much organization is implemented in. You can choose to either donate, sell, or throw away the items, just make sure that you get rid of as much as possible so the organization can begin.

Once your home is starting to look a little better, make sure that you give every item that you still have its own place. This not only makes the area look nicer and cleaner, as well as more organized, but it can do wonders for helping you to remember where things go so it's easier to find them later on. Try not to relapse when it comes to this, by cluttering up the newly cleared space with other things in the future.

Eating Well

The next thing that you can work on is making sure that you follow a diet that is healthy and full of nutrients that are good for you. The typical American diet is not good for the brain, as it doesn't feed the brain what it needs to work at its maximum capacity. The diet has even been proven to cause people higher levels of mental distress.

If you are currently on a diet that is high in sugars, carbs, bad fats, processed foods, and lots and lots of calories, like the typical American diet, then it is time to make some changes.

First, make sure that you take in plenty of healthy fruits and vegetables to start things off. There are many options that you can go with, and the more variety that you are able to add to your diet, the better. Fresh produce—and even the frozen variety—is full of great vitamins and minerals that can help your whole body function properly, and not just the brain.

You should always make sure that you take in lots of healthy carbs. There are some diet plans out right now that focus on how bad carbs can be for you, and how you should avoid them. This is somewhat true, as there are bad carbs out there, such as those found in baked goods and processed foods. But this doesn't mean that all carbs are bad. They can provide you with the sustainable energy that you need to keep going through the day.

Protein is also an important thing you need to consider. Try to take in healthy and lean sources of protein, like hamburger, chicken, turkey, and fish to get the protein and the healthy omega-3 fatty acids that the brain needs to keep your brain healthy. Try to get a few servings of this into your day and into each meal as well.

Dairy products are also an option. These products can make great snacks and provide you with calcium as well as protein. Maybe not the best option for those who are lactose intolerant, though there still is other alternatives such as things like coconut & soy milk etc.

Sleeping Well

It is important that you take the time to get plenty of sleep when you are trying to improve your memory. You will never see results if you only spend four to five hours a night, or even less, sleeping each and every night. This is in addition to feeling worn out, tired, and having lots of cravings for unhealthy foods. So much of our wellbeing is tied to getting enough sleep each night, but most of us are sorely lacking in it.

Sleeping will allow the mind to rejuvenate and rebuild. It lets the mind take all of the images, and events that has happened during that day, and selects those that are important for long term storage. Anything else will just get disregarded.

When the mind is not given enough sleep to let this process occur, then this is something that can affect your ability to remember things. Not only are you tired and worn out, but the brain hasn't been given enough time to store the memories or get rid of any.

If you are dealing with problems with your memories, then it may be time to consider changing up the sleep patterns that you have—and usually, this means that you need to start getting more sleep into your evenings. It is best to get about eight to nine hours of sleep each day so your brain is fully optimal. There are several things that you can do to make sure that you are getting the right amount of sleep each evening including:

1. Setting a bedtime to stick to. You will find that setting your own bedtime, and then sticking with it each and every night, can help you to get enough sleep. Figure out what time you need to be up in the morning, and then pick

out a bedtime that is at least eight hours before that. Stick with it all the time to ensure that you are getting the amount of sleep that your brain needs.

2. Work on a bedtime routine: A bedtime routine can help you to get the best results when it comes to falling asleep easier. This routine is going to signal to the brain that you are getting ready for bed so that it starts to wind down and is ready by the time you get yourself into bed. The bedtime routine doesn't have to take much time. Doing something simple like turning off the TV, brushing your teeth, getting into your pajamas, and reading for fifteen minutes can be exactly what you need to help shut the mind down for the night.

3. Turning off the lights: It is best for you to sleep in the dark. This is beneficial to the brain because it ensures that you are able to get to sleep. The brain is going to react based on whether it is light or dark. If you leave a lot of light near your room at night, the brain may think that it is daytime, and you won't be able to sleep as well. Keep the room as dark as possible to facilitate the best sleep possible.

4. Limit screen time: The more that you can limit screen time before you head to bed, the better off you will be. The blue light that comes off your computer screen can make it really hard to fall asleep and studies have shown that it can definitely mess with REM sleep. It is best to turn off the computer and the television at least an hour before bed to give your brain a break and do something that can help you relax a little bit before you try to go to sleep. Also try wearing anti blue light emitting glasses if you spend a lot of time in front of the screen.
5. Try reading: Taking ten or fifteen minutes to read a little bit before you go to bed. This gives you a chance to calm the mind down and can be relaxing as well. Don't get into something that is too deep because this may have the reverse effect on you and make you stay up for longer. But finding something light and easy to read can be the thing you need to turn off the brain and makes it easier for you to fall asleep.
6. Play relaxing music. If you have trouble getting to sleep at night, make sure that you keep the television off. There are a lot of people who think that they need to keep the television on,

but this is one of the worst things to do as it can really mess with your sleep cycle. If you find that you need some noise to get to sleep, consider getting some soft music to help. You can use classical music or even some quiet nature sounds to help you drift off.

Medications That Can Help with Memory Improvement

There are many people who are worried about their memory and how strong their brains actually are. People will try to make sure that they are doing everything possible to keep their brains sharp and to ensure that they don't have to worry about a host of neurological issues like dementia and Alzheimer's. If you feel that you need to do that bit extra to help support your brain, then you may be interested in looking to see if there are any supplements or other options to help with this.

But the biggest problem today with prescription drugs is that they normally come with a price tag, and they are often not as effective as they seem during a short window of time. This makes it hard for a lot of people to justify having them in the first place, causing them to just forgo them, or look for other options.

If you are looking for a supplement that will be able to help improve your memory, then you do need to be careful. There are some options that can be really helpful when it comes improving your memory, but many of them lack the right chemicals or research behind them to back up their claims.

When taking a supplement for your brain, you want to make sure that you are going with something that will actually work.

For example, there are a number of memory supplements on the market today that can potentially help the brain and memory. Some of the supplements that you should consider include:

- ❖ **Omega-3 fatty acids:** These are the lovely fats that come in fish oil supplements, and they have gained a lot of interest in recent years. You can find these in foods like cold water fish, oils, and some types of walnuts. This fatty acid has been linked to a lower risk of Alzheimer's in many individuals. There still needs to be more studies done to compare the Omega-3's to a placebo to ensure that this is something that is actually beneficial for this disorder.
- ❖ **Huperzine A:** This is sometimes known as Chinese club moss. It is a natural medicine that

can often work in the body similar to how various Alzheimer's drugs do. There are a few questions about how safe and effective it is though.

- ❖ **Acetyle-L-carnitine:** There are some studies that will show how this type of amino acid can be beneficial in helping Alzheimer's patients with various memory problems. It can sometimes provide a great benefit to people with early onset and a fast rate of the disease.
- ❖ **Vitamin E:** This vitamin can be useful in helping slow the progression of Alzheimer's. There has been recent studies that raised concerns about an increased risk of deaths in those who are unhealthy who start to take high doses of this vitamin. If you are worried about this, make sure that you talk to your doctor before you take this kind of supplement.
- ❖ **Asian ginseng:** This is a herb that can be used together with ginkgo biloba, which can help with your quality of life and fatigue. But there does need to be more studies done to prove whether or not this supplement is effective or not.

Chapter 5
Rebooting and Refreshing Your Brain

While the exercises that we talked about in this guide are going to do wonders for helping you increase the memory that you have, there are going to be times when you need to go through and reboot and refresh the brain—and one of the ways that you can do this is to work on the focus that your brain has. No matter how hard we try, there are going to be times when our focus isn't at its best.

There are many things that you can do to help you reboot and refresh the focus that your brain has on a daily basis. This chapter is going to look at some of the simple tasks that you can do, and most of them will only take a few minutes in order to make this goal a reality.

Mindfulness

Mindfulness and meditation are some of the best things that you can do no matter what your overall goals are. Whether you want to make sure that you see a reduction in the amount of stress that you feel, or if you would like to work on clearing the mind, slowing things down, or working on your memory, you will find that mindfulness is one of the best tools to work with.

Buddhists have been practicing mindfulness for centuries in order to experience the present that they live in with more balance. Working with mindfulness can help you to do that, while also increasing your focus and your concentration. When you spend time doing exercises related to mindfulness, you will learn how to direct all your focus and attention to a particular activity. Usually, this is a very simple activity, such as eating or smiling.

Let's say that you choose to focus your attention for a few minutes on smiling. To do this, you can sit with your eyes closed, and then do a slow smile. Make sure that you pay close attention to the different muscles of the face and how it moves when you smile. You feel the sensations on the lips, how the muscles tighten or relax.

Your goal here is to bring attention over to the smiling if the mind does tend to wander off. You can end the focusing session after five minutes, but take a moment when you are done to reflect a bit on how that exercise felt.

Visual Tasks

Visual tasks are so important to the brain, and any time that you are able to tie information that you should remember to a visual, it is much easier for you to remember it. Attending to some kind of visual task can cause some firings in the visual cortex region of your brain. What this means is that these firings can help you keep out some of the distractions that you are facing and helps with focus.

According to Dr. Daniel T. Moore, you may be able to improve your concentration as well as your focus with a visual exercise that utilizes colored pencils. You will need to set your own timer, one that goes off at multiple random time intervals over five minutes. So, this may mean that the alarm is going to sounds after five seconds, and then again after 15, 10, and five.

When the timer is set, you can hold one pencil in each hand, making sure they are about 16 inches from the face and keep them shoulder-width apart. You need to focus exclusively on one of the pencils. Then, when the alarm does sound, you will want to focus the attention on the other. Switch where your focus is between the two pencils each time that you hear the alarm sound.

This is just one example of what you can do when it comes to working with a visual task. You may also find that working with other visuals can help as well. We discussed a number of these previously, but using your home as a way to store information, or adding a picture to the person when you remember their name can help you to remember them better than before.

Chewing Gum

Another thing that you may want to try out is to chew gum. The reason that this works is that the process of chewing gum can help you to use the attentional regions of the brain. This is a simple exercise where you will chew gum when you are doing a task that is work oriented or requires the brain to think when you are learning. This may include doing tasks like homework or attending a lecture with a lot of important information to remember.

Chewing gum has been shown to help students and others improve their ability to learn, and help them to retain and then retrieve the information that they need. An example that studies have shown that students who chewed gum while doing various math activities for a total of 14 weeks were able to achieve tests scores that were higher to those who didn't chew gum at all.

According to this study, which was done by the Baylor College of Medicine, the students who chewed gum were able to score about 24 and 36 percent higher than those who didn't chew gum on immediate word recall tests and delayed word recall tests respectively.

It has been proven in many studies that chewing gum actually helps with visual memory tasks and long- term concentration.

Belly Breathing

Sometimes the issue that you are dealing with is the fact that you are not breathing in the most efficient manner. Inefficient patterns in breathing can sometimes suppress how well you are able to focus and concentrate. This is because you may be limiting the amount of oxygen that enter your brain. If this is a problem you may think you have, then working on exercises that are known as belly breathing can sometimes help to improve your concentration and focus simply by correcting your patterns of breathing.

Belly breathing can help with things like boosting your IQ, providing more oxygen to the brain, and improving your learning efficiency.

To do this process, you just need to place one hand on your stomach and then inhale slowly through your nose, and into your stomach. You want to let the stomach expand for three seconds or so. After that time has passed, you can exhale for an additional three seconds, using your stomach muscles to push out the breath, rather than your diaphragm or your lungs. Spend at least a few minutes doing this, making sure that your stomach muscles do the work with the exhalation, to get the best results.

If you work on increasing your memory and using the various techniques that are out there to do this, then you will find that your focus is automatically going to increase as well. However, there are still going to be times when the focus and concentration you need will still be lacking. Working with some of the tasks and exercises above can help you get your focus back on track so that you can see the best results.

Conclusion

Thank you for making it through to the end of Memory Improvement! Let's hope it was informative and able to provide you with all of the tools you need to achieve your goals—whatever they may be.

Burt remember, our memories aren't fading because we are aging or because of things that we can't control. Oftentimes, the issue is because we just aren't challenging the brain and putting it to work. When this happens, the mind is going to start deteriorating, causing us to have the trouble remembering some of the very basic things that go on in our day. However, as we start to stimulate the brain more and get it to learn new things, or try something we have never tried before, then our memories will start to improve at the same time.

Dealing with a failing memory can be a difficult task. But in this book we have covered the basics of what you need to know about the memory, why it is important, and effective techniques and methods that you can apply to start improving your memory gradually.

Increasing our memories ability is something we all want to improve, and something we all can do. So, make sure to take all the essential lessons and information you have learnt and apply it to your daily life.

www.ingramcontent.com/pod-product-compliance
Lightning Source LLC
Chambersburg PA
CBHW081226080526
44587CB00022B/3843